Baedeker's

HONG KONG

Imprint

Cover picture: Aberdeen

54 colour photographs
3 general maps, 2 plans, 1 transport plan, 2 town plans

Text:
Detlef CH. Biehn, Hong Kong

Conception and editorial work:
Redaktionsbüro Harenberg, Schwerte
English language: Alec Court

Cartography:
Ingenieurbüro für Kartographie Huber & Oberländer, Munich
Hong Kong Government, Department of Lands, Survey and Town Planning (plan of Hong Kong and Kowloon)

General direction:
Dr Peter Baumgarten, Baedeker Stuttgart

English translation:
James Hogarth

Source of illustrations:
Biehn (21), dpa (19), Hong Kong Tourist Association (11), Mauritius (1), Portuguese National Tourist Office (1), Storto (1)

Following the tradition established by Karl Baedeker in 1844, sights of particular interest and hotels of outstanding quality are distinguished by either one or two asterisks.

To make it easier to locate the various sights listed in the "A to Z" section of the Guide, their coordinates on the large city plan at the end of the book are shown in blue (for Hong Kong) or red (for Kowloon) at the head of each entry.

Only a selection of hotels, restaurants and shops can be given: no reflection is implied, therefore, on establishments not included.

In a time of rapid change it is difficult to ensure that all the information given is entirely accurate and up to date, and the possibility of error can never be entirely eliminated. Although the publishers can accept no responsibility for inaccuracies and omissions they are always grateful for corrections and suggestions for improvement.

US and Canadian edition
Prentice Hall Press

Licensed user:
Mairs Geographischer Verlag GmbH & Co., Ostfildern-Kemnat bei Stuttgart

Reproductions:
Gölz Repro-Service GmbH, Ludwigsburg

The name *Baedeker* is a registered trademark

Printed in Great Britain by Jarrold & Sons Ltd Norwich

0 86145 213 5 UK
0–13–058009–0 US & Canada

Contents

Baedeker Hong Kong

Preface

This Pocket Guide to Hong Kong is one of the new generation of Baedeker city guides.

Baedeker pocket guides, illustrated throughout in colour, are designed to meet the needs of the modern traveller. They are quick and easy to consult, with the principal sights described in alphabetical order and practical details about opening times, how to get there, etc., shown in the margin.

Each guide is divided into three parts. The first part gives a general account of the city, its history, population, culture and so on; in the second part the principal sights are described; and the third part contains a variety of practical information designed to help visitors to find their way about and make the most of their stay.

The new guides are abundantly illustrated and contain numbers of newly drawn plans. At the back of the book is a large city map, and each entry in the main part of the guide gives the coordinates of the square on the map in which the particular feature can be located. Users of this guide, therefore will have no difficulty in finding what they want to see.

HYF

Facts and Figures

General

Territory

Hong Kong (Xiang Gang in Pinyin Chinese transliteration) is a British Crown Colony. The name Hong Kong – Chinese for "fragrant harbor" – is applied both to the Crown Colony as a whole, which is now also called "a dependent territory", and to the small island lying off the mainland opposite the Kowloon peninsula.

Language

The official languages of Hong Kong are English and (since 1974) Cantonese. 82 per cent of the inhabitants speak Chinese in the Cantonese dialect, which is understood by 95 per cent of the population.

Script

The Chinese script in which the language and its various dialects are written is an extraordinary cultural achievement, developed some 4000 years ago out of an ideographic script then in use. It now consists of over 7000 characters, and for the purposes of everyday life it is necessary to know about half of these. Attempts are being made in the People's Republic of China to simplify the script in order to make it easier to use.

Capital

Victoria, in the north of the central part of Hong Kong Island and nowadays generally known as its Central District, is the capital of the colony and its commercial center.

Situation

Hong Kong lies off the South China coast in the Pearl River Estuary, which can be as much as 19 miles/30 km wide. Just south of the Tropic of Cancer, it is between latitude 22° 9′ and

◀ *Hong Kong – where junks coexist with skyscrapers*

22° 37′ N and between longitude 113° 62′ and 114° 30′ E. It is bounded on the north by the Chinese province of Canton (Guandong) and on the south by the South China Sea.
Long stretches of the coast are difficult to get to because of their natural geographical inaccessibility, and changes in the level of the land and in sea-level have left behind the maze of islands and remote bays which is characteristic of Hong Kong. The rounded granite cliffs, a continuation of the South China Highlands, and steep slopes make the coastal region a delightful landscape. Once the slopes were covered in trees but now they have only scrub and stunted conifers. Among the numerous tropical plants are pink azaleas and the famous Hong Kong orchid (*Bauhinia blakeana*), the official emblem of the British Crown Colony.

Climate

Because of its geographical position Hong Kong has a subtropical climate with rain in summer because of the north-east or south-east monsoon. Ninety per cent of the annual rainfall – which can take the form of torrential downpours – is in the months of April to September. The summers are hot and humid, and the winters are cool, though dry and sunny. Spring and autumn are very brief. The average difference between day and night-time temperatures is as little as 10 °F/5·5 °C. Day-time temperatures in summer generally range between 77 and 88 °F/25 and 31 °C, and the humidity, which can often be as high as 90 per cent, makes this a climatically oppressive time of the year. Between May and September Hong Kong is often hit by typhoons ("great wind" in Chinese).
In winter the temperature rarely drops below 50 °F/10 °C, and on fine days it may climb to over 68 °F/20 °C. The most pleasant time of year for a visit is October–December, when there are blue skies and pleasantly hot sunshine.

Area and population

Hong Kong has an area of 409 sq. miles/1066 sq. km. Most of the population is concentrated in the area of Hong Kong, Kowloon and, increasingly, the New Towns in the New Territories. The Crown Colony has the highest population density in the world, with an average of 12,700 to the sq. mile (4972 to the sq. km), rising to 43,500 to the sq. mile (15,000 to the sq. km) in Hong Kong, 252,300 to the sq. mile (87,000 to the sq. km) in Kowloon, and no less than 479,775 to the sq. mile (165,440 to the sq. km) in Sham Shui Po (New Kowloon), though in the New Territories it is only 2300 to the sq. mile (792 to the sq. km); this may be compared with 23,680 to the sq. mile (8200 to the sq. km) for London. Official figures put Hong Kong's population at 5·3 million in 1983 (98 per cent of these being Chinese), but more realistic estimates make it about 6·2 million. The annual growth rate of about 2·2 per cent is due not so much to high birth rates as to immigration. Time after time legal and illegal immigrants, together with refugees from China and East Asian trouble spots, have poured into the Crown Colony. Between 1949 and 1980 alone, over 1·1 million Chinese settled in Hong Kong illegally. Despite all their efforts the British authorities have failed to solve the refugee problem satisfactorily, and more than 1 million people live in households of over 7 to a room, about half a million are in slums on the granite hillsides, and, in the bays where they are safe from typhoons, there are 100,000 "boat people". The average age in 1983 was 26, with 33·6 per cent of the population under 20, and only 7·1 per cent over 65.

City districts

Hong Kong is made up of the actual island of Hong Kong, with its administrative center Victoria (once a city in its own right but now the "Central District"), the peninsula of Kowloon (meaning "nine dragons"), with the urban area of the same name, and the New Territories which are still quite rural and include most of the colony's 236 islands.
Each of these areas is divided into districts, each with a district office.
The island of Hong Kong has four districts – Central and Western, Eastern, Southern and Wan Chai.
Kowloon has six districts – Kowloon City, Kwun Tong, Mong Kok, Sham Shui Po, Wong Tai Sin and Yau Ma Tei.
The New Territories are divided into eight districts – the Islands, North, Sai Kung, Sha Tin, Tai Po, Tsuen Wan, Tuen Mun and Yuen Long.
The various districts are in turn divided into two or three sub-districts in which there are branches of the district offices. Thus Tsim Sha Tsui, the business center of Kowloon, belongs to the district of Kowloon City, while Kennedy Town on the island of Hong Kong belongs to the Central and Western district.

Administration

Hong Kong has a governor appointed by the Queen who is her representative and head of the executive. There is a Legislative Council (locally referred to as "LegCo") of not more than 54 members, including the governor and 4 ex-officio members, 23 other official members and 27 unofficial members; at present the Council has 22 official and 26 unofficial members. Laws are enacted by the governor (currently Sir Edward Youde) with the advice and consent of the Legislative Council.
The governor presides over an Executive Council (known as "ExCo") of five ex-officio members, one official and nine unofficial members, all appointed by him.
The city is administered by an Urban Council of 24 members, 12 appointed by the governor and the others elected for a four-year term (with the possibility of re-election). The council elects the mayor, who may be either an elected or an appointed member or a candidate from outside the council.

Population and Religion

Population

At Hong Kong's first census in 1851 it had a population of 32,983, of whom 31,463 were Chinese. In 1931 the population was 878,947, including 859,425 Chinese. The present population can only be estimated, but a figure of 6 million is probably not far from the truth. Some 98 per cent of the population are Chinese, predominantly of Cantonese stock; the next largest groups are Sze Yap and Chiu Chow. The rest of the population consists of Caucasians and Asians, including about 60,000 from Commonwealth countries (24,000 British, 14,000 Indians, 7700 Pakistanis), 12,000 Americans, 7100 Japanese, 2200 Germans and 1400 French.
Hong Kong is a racially very mixed yet notably tolerant society. The Chinese are a proud people with ancient traditions and a great cultural heritage, as are the Caucasians. Like the non-Chinese minority, they tend to keep themselves to themselves, each respecting the other, but intermarriage between Chinese and non-Chinese is relatively common.

Faces of Asia

Hong Kong was and is a magnet for illegal immigrants from the People's Republic of China and East Asian countries that have been affected by crises, as happened in 1937 during the Sino–Japanese War, in 1949 when the People's Republic was being founded, from 1966 to 1969 during the Cultural Revolution, and at the time of the war in Vietnam (80 per cent of the Vietnamese "boat people" were Chinese). The refugee problem is an enormous burden on the city. Although under the Resettlement Program about 2 million people were moved from refugee camps into public housing estates between 1953 and 1980, the British authorities were swamped by the great influx of refugees. In 1979, for example, Hong Kong took in 73,300

Vietnamese refugees, and by 1981 24,000 were still waiting to be resettled overseas.
Radical immigration laws were introduced in November 1980, since when only 150 "legal" immigrants a day are officially allowed in, and they must be able to prove that they already have a close relative in the Colony. This measure, which followed consultation with the provincial government in Kwantung, proved necessary after the average monthly influx into Hong Kong from China had reached 12,000. This also marked the end of the arrangement whereby any refugee who managed to reach the city was entitled to apply for a permit to stay. The punishment for helping illegal immigrants is now a year's imprisonment.

Squatter people

"Squatter people" is the name given to some half a million people, mainly immigrants from China, who live in slums on the hillsides or in shanty towns on stilts at the water-side, because they are too poor to afford proper accommodations. As well as these squatters on land and in the shanty towns, there are also the "tanka", the 100,000 squatters who live on board boats packed tightly together in the typhoon havens at Aberdeen, Yaumati and Causeway Bay. Their numbers have fallen by about 20 per cent since 1976 because of the government's intensive home-building programme. This means that because Hong Kong is a city that can no longer expand outwards and can only go up, even the slums on the hillsides are having to be cleared to provide sites for more high-rise buildings.

Religion

In Hong Kong temples, churches, mosques and synagogues happily co-exist side by side. All the world's great religions are represented here. Buddhism and Taoism have the greatest following, and there are no fewer than 600 temples for the followers of these two religious philosophies.

Confucius

The influence and impact of Confucius ("Master K'ung", 551–479 B.C.) on Chinese culture are significant. The teaching of Confucius is based on the religious idea that adopting a correct attitude can lead to harmony with the eternal order of the cosmos. This attitude, he taught, consists in loyalty to the self and to others, altruism, humaneness, righteousness, decorum, wisdom and uprightness. In China and in South East Asia in general the aristocratic teaching of Confucius with regard to public and private behaviour constituted a norm from the time of the Han dynasty (206 B.C.–A.D. 220) for several centuries onwards. The "five relationships" – between prince and subject, father and son, man and wife, elder and younger brothers, friend and friend – were founded on the virtues of love for one's fellow men, justice and respect. An expression of these is respect for one's inheritance, for rites and for music, and this continues even after death (veneration of ancestors).
The validity and significance of the moral maxims of Confucius have remained the subject of lively debate right up to the present day. Unlike Buddhism and Christianity, Confucianism and Taoism, which was founded by Lao-tse, did not develop into major world religions, but long remained virtually unknown outside their country of origin.

Lao-tse

In Taoism, which developed later than Confucianism, the life of the philosopher Lao-tse ("Old Master", 4th–3rd c. B.C.) was elaborated into a legend according to which Lao-tse did not die but journeyed off toward the West where he entrusted the book "Tao Teching" to the guard at the frontier pass. The aphoristic series made up of 81 short sections is concerned with "Tao" (the basis of the cosmos) and its vital force "Te" which the wise man may obtain by profound meditation on the "Tao". Harmony with it may be attained only by refraining from all activity ("wu wei" in Chinese) and by abstaining from any involvement in worldly affairs. The unique combination of intellectual depth and linguistic simplicity has led to more than 130 translations of what has become the best-known work in Chinese philosophical literature.

Philosophical Taoism developed in the 4th and 3rd c. B.C. in the context of Chinese philosophical speculation about the basic nature of the cosmos ("Tao"). It is distinct from Taoism as a religion which sought the prolongation of life and the immortality of the body by means of meditation, diet, alchemy, gymnastics and sexual practices. Since as far back as the 2nd c. B.C. there have been set religious practices which were subsequently competing with the new force of Buddhism. Nowadays popular Taoism is a sort of syncretic system of popular beliefs within which some of the gods of old-style Taoism still live on. The philosophy of Taoism, on the other hand, has had its disciples right up until the present day and has at times strongly influenced poetry. It also has its adherents in the West as well as in the East among the adepts of the Chinese art of defence known as kung fu, which is largely based on the principles of Taoism.

Yin and Yang

The doctrine of the cosmic principles of Yin and Yang (in Chinese "dark" and "light"), under which all beings may be subsumed, has been part of the Chinese spiritual heritage since the 5th–3rd c. B.C. Yin and Yang symbolize two forces, complementary to one another and dependent on one another which are constantly in motion in our universe. They are looked upon as two parts of an indivisible whole, mutually inclusive of each other, each of which has within itself the qualities of its complement. They do not represent so much cause and effect as sound and its echo, or light and shade. Yin stands for the feminine (the negative, the earth, submissiveness, unreality, passivity, goodness), whereas Yang stands for the masculine (the positive, the sun, resolution, reality, activity). Yin and Yang also play a big part in Chinese medicine and alchemy.

Buddhism

Buddhism began its expansion into lands outside India from the 3rd c. B.C. onward. As it did so it underwent manifold changes with its assimilation into popular religions. While Hinajana Buddhism remained true to the doctrine of Buddha and recognized neither a personal soul nor a god, Mahajana Buddhism, the form of Buddhism that became the great world religion, adopted the cult of the mortal gods as well. It was under the Han dynasty (about A.D. 65) that Buddhism won its first disciples in China. The majority of the present population of Hong Kong profess the doctrine of Lao-tse (Taoism) and the religion of Mahajana Buddhism.

Around 500,000 people in Hong Kong are Christians, either Protestants or Roman Catholics. The 260,000 Catholics can choose between 310 Catholic schools, 11 religious communities, and 64 chapels and churches. There are nearly 600

A shanty town of the squatter people ▶

Ching Chuen Koong – a Taoist temple

In the harbor, Hong Kong Island

congregations of Protestants, with 380 elementary and secondary schools, and two colleges.
Other religions include Islam (30,000), Hinduism (8000) and Animism. Hong Kong's Jewish community numbers about 500.

Transport

The port

Hong Kong's nerve center is Victoria Harbour between the island of Hong Kong and the Kowloon Peninsula. It varies in width between 1 and 6 miles/1·6 and 9·6 km and covers an area of some 15,000 acres/6000 hectares. It is one of the finest natural harbors in the world and is well up the international league in terms of tonnage handled. Its Kwai Chung computerized container terminal is the third largest in the world, handling 367,997 units in 1984. Most ships berth in the Middle Harbour, but large liners generally have to use the Ocean Terminal in Kowloon. Much of the city's passenger traffic is carried by water (over 7·7 million passengers in 1984). Ferry-boats, hydrofoils and hovercraft carry passengers and motor vehicles between Hong Kong and Kowloon, the Islands and Macau.

Airport

Hong Kong's international airport at Kai Tak is always being enlarged and its runways are built right out into Kowloon Bay. Traffic is increasing at a faster rate than for any other airport in South East Asia. Its capacity for freight (420,000+ in 1985) is to be expanded, together with its annual passenger handling capacity which was 12 million in 1985 and is to be increased to 18 million. There are 1000 scheduled flights by 34 airlines in and out of Hong Kong every week, and direct services, sometimes with stop-overs, fly to many European destinations, such as Amsterdam, Frankfurt, Geneva, London, Paris, Rome and Zürich. Within Asia itself there are direct flights to all major airports. Arrival at, or departure from, Hong Kong's airport is quite an experience. The airplane passes only a few feet above the blocks of apartments immediately adjoining the airport, and there is a breath-taking view as it flies between the island of Hong Kong and Kowloon and approaches the runway built out into the sea.

Railroad and Underground Services

Hong Kong has only one railroad line. It was electrified in 1983 and runs from Hung Hom Station in Kowloon to the Chinese city of Canton (Guangzhou). After a break of 30 years direct daily services were started again in 1979 and there are three through trains a day to the Chinese mainland. The journey to Canton takes 3 hours 20 minutes. The Kowloon–Canton Railway Corporation coaches have air-conditioned first and second class compartments but the trains on Sundays and holidays are often hopelessly overcrowded. For other destinations, such as the planned direct route from Hong Kong via Shanghai to Peking, or to connect up with the Trans-Siberian or Orient Express, it is necessary to change trains at the frontier station of Lo Wu. This line also carries considerable freight traffic, and foodstuffs from China reach Hong Kong's markets by this route every day.
A fully air-conditioned underground railroad, the MTR (Mass Transport Railway), links Hong Kong Island (Central Station,

Chaiwan) with the districts of Kwun Tong and Tsuen Wan in Kowloon. A road and rail tunnel between Quarry Bay and Cha Kow Ling is due to come into operation in 1989.

Trams

There has been a tram service along the north shore of Hong Kong Island since 1904. The line runs for 19 miles/39·4 km, passing through North Point, Wan Chai, Central and Kennedy Town.

Peak Tramway

The famous Peak Tramway, opened in 1888, is a funicular running between Garden Road and Victoria Peak, the highest point on Hong Kong Island (1818 ft/554 m). On the way up, which takes 8 minutes with 5 stops, there are magnificent views of the city and the harbor.

Buses

Buses that run from 6 a.m. to midnight provide very cheap transport virtually throughout Hong Kong.

Highways and Trunk Roads

Hong Kong has no urban highways of the Western European type, although some sections of road in Kowloon and the New Territories are of similar standard, such as the expressways from Tuen Mun (New Territories) to Kowloon, from Kowloon to Sha Tin and Kwun Tong, the section between Causeway Bay and Taikoo Shing (Hong Kong Island) and out to Sai Kung, as well as under the harbor between Kowloon and Hong Kong Island and continuing into the Cross-Harbour Tunnel.

Hong Kong has about 730 miles/1200 km of roads and at least 435 licensed vehicles to every mile (270 per km). It's no wonder that Hong Kong's roads are always congested.

Expressway in Hong Kong

A 150 mile/240 km long highway linking Hong Kong and Macau is still under construction. Just under half the highway that is due to run for 5 miles/8·2 km along the north coast of Hong Kong Island has recently been opened to traffic.
Major roads leading to the destinations shown:

Hong Kong Island

Stubbs Road: Repulse Bay, Stanley, Aberdeen, Shek O
Garden Road: Peak
Hennessy Road: eastern districts
Queen's Road West: western districts
Gloucester Road: Cross-Harbour Tunnel

Kowloon

Chatham Road: Airport, Cross-Harbour Tunnel
Waterloo Road: New Territories
Salisbury Road: Sha Tsui (Kowloon City), Cross-Harbour Tunnel

New Territories

Waterloo Road, Lion Rock Tunnel Road: Sha Tin, Tai Po, Fan Ling
Chatham Road, To Kwa Wan Road, Clear Water Bay Road: Clear Water Bay, Sai Kung
Waterloo Road, Boundary Street, Castle Peak Road: western New Territories (Tsuen Wan, Tuen Mun, Yuen Long, Kam Tin)

Culture

The role that Hong Kong plays within Asia is in every way a very individual one. With its vivid mixture of races the Crown Colony is perhaps the most cosmopolitan of all cities and it can look back on a Chinese cultural tradition which has its roots in the Hsia dynasty about the middle of the third millennium B.C.
It has a fascinating landscape, with Victoria Peak set amid green hills and Kowloon's mountain chain of the Nine Dragons, rising out of the typical big-city smog into an azure sky or, in the dry season, veiled in thick cloud. It has delightful islands with deserted sandy beaches, lakes set in verdant valleys, and spectacular mountain roads with breath-taking views. All this is in sharp contrast to the modern backdrop of high-rise building with skyscrapers soaring up to 66 stories high, and hopelessly overcrowded slums. Hong Kong puts on many faces – Chinese markets that are a riot of color, ancient temples and pagodas reeking of joss-sticks, giants on its skyline, ugly industrial estates, shanty towns, no-go areas, prosperous suburbs in Victoria and Kowloon with their villas and their high society, or districts where the shopfronts and houses recall the Chinese seaboard towns of the 19th c. And everywhere is swarming with people, and there is so very much noise. It takes time to assimilate and understand this host of impressions, to discover the charm of these contradictions and comprehend all that seems so extraordinary.
Immigrants from other Asiatic countries, Europe and America, and a century under British rule, have not managed fundamentally to alter the old Chinese way of thinking with so many thousand years behind it. Mindful of tradition, people keep up their cultural heritage in their everyday life, as, for example, they celebrate their annual festivals. Thus it is, in a city whose pace is fast and furious and which seems on the point of bursting for lack of space, the sale of modern hi-tech computers has not put

a stop to using the age-old abacus for totting up the bill for the shopping. At the Chinese New Year the red paper flags of the household gods flutter directly above electronic cameras, and car number-plates with Chinese symbols for long life and happiness are much sought after. In this "Manhattan of the Orient" everything may seem to be ordered on Western lines, but its soul remains Chinese. Hong Kong is a city of superlatives. It has the world's most expensive office building (the Hong Kong Shanghai Bank), the longest escalator, the most Rolls Royces, and over 100,000 "undeclared" millionaires, while hundreds of thousands live in pitiful squalor. Hong Kong is the world's biggest exporter of textiles, toys, radios and watches, and its third largest financial center.

In the country districts of the New Territories Hong Kong still has pretty and unspoilt spots, with sights that are worth seeing. In the fields water-buffaloes can still be seen pulling the plough, and the Chinese eating-houses have kept their old ways and customs. Although these parts, too, are increasingly being swamped by the influence of imported Western commercial culture, the New Territories still offer an alternative for the visitor who is interested in something else beside shopping.

Every evening one can sample the atmosphere of old China in the many movie theaters showing Mandarin movies, or through the Chinese opera put out regularly on radio and TV, as well as during the colorful traditional festivals that are celebrated in great style every year.

The people of Hong Kong are incredibly energetic, and brimming over with vitality. Any talk of Oriental impassivity is totally out of place. Hong Kong is in fact where East meets West, where Asia is leavened with a European yeast.

Hong Kong as a cultural center

In recent years Hong Kong has established itself as one of the leading cultural centers of East and South-East Asia. The Hong Kong Philharmonic Orchestra and the Hong Kong Chinese Orchestra have a firm place in the life of the city. The Arts Centre, City Hall, the Queen Elizabeth and Macpherson stadiums, the A.C. Hall, Tsuen Wan Town Hall, Ko Shan (open-air) Theatre, Lee Theatre and the Coliseum, shaped like a huge mushroom, offer a full program of events using local artists as well as soloists and ensembles from abroad. Evidence of the growing interest in the arts is provided by the Asian Arts Festival, the Hong Kong Film Festival and other festivals with various themes, such as children's choirs or puppet plays. A whole range of galleries, libraries, museums, and foreign cultural institutes provide facilities where locals and visitors alike can enjoy both educational pursuits and the arts.

Universities

The University of Hong Kong, founded in 1911, has 7000 students in its five faculties and three schools. The Chinese University of Hong Kong in Sha Tin (New Territories) was founded in 1963, and consists of three colleges, with four faculties and 5200 matriculated students. The teaching is mainly in Cantonese. The Hong Kong Polytechnic, established in 1972, has 19 teaching departments grouped under four divisions with 8000 full-time, 4700 part-time and 13,300 evening students.

In addition to these degree-awarding higher educational establishments Hong Kong has a number of technical and vocational schools and colleges as well as a music academy, the Hong Kong Conservatory of Music.

University of Hong Kong

Academy of Ballet

The Hong Kong Academy of Ballet was established in 1979.

Libraries

The library of the University of Hong Kong contains 580,000 volumes, that of the Chinese University 645,000; there are 19 public libraries with a total of 1·1 million volumes; and the various foreign cultural institutes also have substantial libraries.

Art

Chinese artistic achievement is particularly notable in the fields of wood-, ivory- and jade-carving, porcelain, pottery and sculpture, carpets, ink-wash painting and, above all, calligraphy. Nowadays typical examples of local craftwork can come from factories in the industrial heart of the city, or from remote villages in the New Territories. In many cases the crafts have been handed down from generation to generation, meaning that many modern artists are able to adapt to traditional stylishness to practical 20th-c. knowhow, or create something entirely new using ancient techniques.

Chinese opera

Chinese opera developed in the 7th c. out of the choral dancing practiced at the Imperial Court in Peking. It calls for a variety of talents in the performers, involving as it does both miming and symbolic dancing, declamation and stylized singing. The participants are heavily made up, with a thick coating of rouge or white paint to symbolize fidelity or power. The sumptuous costumes, brightly colored, indicate the social rank of the character depicted. There are two forms of Chinese opera – the old Peking opera and the newer Cantonese opera, which is very popular in Hong Kong.

Erotic art (netsukes)

Chinese opera, in classical costumes of the Ming period

Theaters and orchestras

The Hong Kong Philharmonic, established in 1973, has developed into an orchestra of international standard. In addition there are the Hong Kong Chinese Orchestra and, for the rising generation of musicians, the Hong Kong Youth Chinese Orchestra and the Hong Kong Youth Symphony Orchestra.
Regular dramatic performances are given in the City Hall by the Hong Kong Repertory Theatre, and other companies also put on productions in the Arts Centre and the City Hall.

Commerce and Industry

Originally the Crown Colony provided the British with access to the Asian mainland and the Chinese with one more trading post. Today Hong Kong has developed into an international financial, commercial and communications center. One hundred and forty international banks have offices in the city, the gold market is the third largest in the world, and 64 countries have accredited diplomats here.
A free market economy and the investment advantages of a free trade zone are guaranteed by the government, and except on tobacco, alcohol and perfume there are no duties or restrictions on imports. Large numbers of foreign firms have been attracted by the *laissez-faire* legislation, an outstanding communications network and the availability of cheap labor, particularly since the immigrants started streaming in.
Hong Kong's total annual trade figure is over £25,000 million, and the People's Republic of China also earns about 40 per cent of its hard currency through Hong Kong since it supplies the Crown Colony with consumer goods, foodstuffs, building materials and a wide range of other goods. The Hong Kong Chinese also send large sums back to their relatives in the People's Republic. A year after China was "opened up" the Chinese People's Congress resolved to establish "Special Economic Zones" which have developed into artificial outposts of the free market-place. The wage-rates and tax benefits have already encouraged 490 firms – several of them from Hong Kong – to move into Shenzen, on the north frontier, to set up joint ventures with the Chinese.
From 1 July 1997, when the 99-year lease of the New Territories runs out, the Crown Colony will pass under Chinese sovereignty under the terms of the Hong Kong Treaty of 29 September 1984, but will retain its special status for a transition period of 50 years (i.e. free market economy, Common Law, freely convertible Hong Kong dollar, existence of the stock exchange and private property, unrestricted freedom to travel, the English language, freedoms of speech, religion and the press, etc.), all of which represents the present capitalist system.
The main economic difficulties are due to the shortage of land, water-supply problems with industrial expansion, and the search for new markets for a constantly growing range of exports.

The local market

As a city state operating as an international commercial center Hong Kong has only a small local market because of its severely limited natural resources.
Some 9·2 per cent of the available land area is used for intensive cultivation (with, for instance, five crops of fresh vegetables a year), and 50 per cent of that has to be artificially irrigated.

Bank of China – an outpost of the People's Republic in Hong Kong

Many of the mostly tenant farmers have managed to increase their yields considerably. Fishing, both in the sea and the river, is very important as a source of protein for the population.
Hong Kong's economy as a whole is centered on importing, exporting and re-exporting. There are a number of chambers of commerce and industrial associations concerned with maintaining the necessary international contacts. The main economic sectors are building, manufacturing, commerce, banking and insurance. In 1985 there was growth in real terms of 7 per cent, and unemployment was 3·5 per cent.

Traditional industries

By far the most jobs (42 per cent) are in textiles and clothing. These are followed by electronics, machine tools and the plastics industries, including the manufacture of toys, a field in which for years Hong Kong has been among the world leaders. Other major sectors are the watchmaking and jewelry industries.
Although most production is by small and medium-sized firms, there is a trend in manufacturing towards high-tech specialization (e.g. in electronic micro-components) as Hong Kong's textiles have been increasingly undercut by the emergence of other cheap producer countries. Growth in textiles is, therefore, getting to be almost exclusively in the top-quality ranges.
The New Territories have two industrial parks, Tai Po and Yuen Long.
Tourism is the third largest foreign exchange earner (£1·6 billion in 1985), and with the completion in 1988 of an international congress center in Wan Chai the number of Hong Kong's hotel rooms will reach 20,000, compared with 18,000 in 1985.

Notable Hong Kong Figures

John Gordon Davis

John Gordon Davis, a writer well known in South-East Asia, some of whose novels are set in Hong Kong, was born in Rhodesia and educated in South Africa. During this time his vacations were spent with the Dutch whaling fleet and on British cargo vessels on the high seas. In 1966 he became public prosecutor in Hong Kong, and made a name for himself in the trials of members of the Chinese secret society known as the Triads.

When his first novel, "Hold my Hand, I'm Dying", became an international best-seller he abandoned the law in favor of writing. Since then he has written four very successful novels – "Typhoon" ("Cape of Storms"), "The Years of the Hungry Tiger", "Taller than Trees" and "Leviathan". He now lives in the south of Spain.

William Jardine (1784–1843)

William Jardine, businessman and politician, started his career as a ship's doctor with the East India Company. In 1819 he founded his first business in Bombay; then in 1827 his interest in the China trade led him to Canton and Macau, where he became the leading businessman in the region. He soon succeeded in breaking the monopoly of the East India Company, managing in face of considerable opposition to ship the first "free" consignment of tea to London.

In 1839 he left Canton and Macau and gave up his business activity in order to become a Member of Parliament. Although he never in fact visited Hong Kong, he ranks as one of the founding fathers of the colony, having played a major part in bringing about the Treaty of Nanking (see History, below). He died at the age of 59.

While in Bombay he joined up with a partner, Nicholas James Sullivan Matheson, who laid the foundations of Jardine Matheson & Co., which grew to be the greatest of Hong Kong's traditional British commercial houses, before transferring its headquarters to the Bahamas in 1985.

Bruce Lee (1940–73)

Bruce Lee was the film actor who made the Chinese martial art of kung fu widely known throughout the world. The new sport was taken up with great enthusiasm, and numbers of kung fu clubs were established.

Bruce Lee was born in San Francisco, the son of a Chinese opera singer, and spent his early years partly in the United States and partly in Hong Kong, where he went to school and college. At the age of 15 he began to take a keen interest in the Chinese art of self-defense known as *wing chun kung fu*, devoting his whole energy to a hard training programme, self-imposed, developing his own ideas and techniques and finally creating his own form of martial art, *jeet kune do*.

In 1961 he began to study philosophy at George Washington University, and founded his first *jeet kune do* school in Seattle. He made his début on television in a thirty-part serial, "The Green Hornet" (1966). His first starring role was in "Fists of Fury" (1970), and thereafter, until his death, one film followed another – "Enter the Dragon", "Return of the Dragon", "The Dragon Dies Hard", etc.

Notable Hong Kong Figures

Yue-Kong Pao
(b. 1918)

Sir Yue-Kong Pao, one of Hong Kong's wealthiest men, heads the World-Wide Shipping Group and is generally accepted as being the biggest private shipowner in the world.

He was born in Chekiang (China), the second of the three sons of a local businessman, and educated in Shanghai. At the age of 22 he went into banking, and worked in this field for ten years; then in 1949 he moved to Hong Kong and at first engaged in the import and export business. In 1955 he made his début as a shipowner with the purchase of a 27-year-old freighter for US $770,000. His fleet now amounts to some 200 vessels with a total tonnage of almost 20 million GRT. The business has branches in Bermuda, Tokyo, London, New York, Singapore and Rio de Janeiro. At the end of 1981 Sir Yue-Kong Pao had US $850 million of ships on order!

Sir Yue-Kong Pao is Chairman of the Eastern Asia Navigation Company, World Maritime Ltd, the World Shipping and Investment Company and World International (Holdings) Ltd, and founder of the World-Wide Sea Training School in Hong Kong, which trains young men for the various types of work on board ship.

He was given an honorary doctorate of law by the University of Hong Kong in 1975 and by the Chinese University of Hong Kong in 1977. In 1976 he was appointed CBE (Commander of the Order of the British Empire) and in 1978 he was knighted.

Henry Pottinger
(1789–1856)

Sir Henry Pottinger, first Governor of Hong Kong, was educated at Belfast Academy, but left school at the age of 12 to go to sea. In 1803 he arrived in India and began to work for the East India Company, returning to England after 27 years of continuous service in the colonies. In 1840 he was selected by the Foreign Secretary, Lord Palmerston, to take over from Charles Elliott, founder of the colony of Hong Kong. From August 1841 to June 1843 he was British administrator in Hong Kong, and then became first Governor of the territory, now officially declared a colony. He held that position until May 1844; then in 1846 he became Governor of the Cape of Good Hope and soon afterwards Governor of Madras. He died in Malta in 1856 on his way home from India.

Run Run Shaw
(b. 1907)

Sir Run Run Shaw has been since 1963 President of the Shaw Brothers Organization, a family firm which he has built up with his brother Runme, who lives in Singapore. The firm owns many movie theaters all over South-East Asia, a film production company in Hong Kong which takes part in many international co-productions and a film company which also operates in the United States and Canada.

In 1959 Sir Run Run came to Hong Kong and built up Shaw Brothers Movie Town, the studios in which are now turning out some 40 films a year. Associated with the complex is an acting school, and there are even dwelling-houses within this film city occupied by some of the 1200 employees and their families.

The film magnate leads a very simple life, practises *tai-chi chuan* (shadow boxing) daily, trains in kung fu, performs Chinese breathing exercises and eats the plainest food. He has a large and handsome villa but uses this only for social occasions, preferring for the most part to live at the studio.

Sir Run Run is a prominent and generous patron of the arts in Hong Kong and is chairman of the Hong Kong Arts Festival Society and the Hong Kong Arts Centre. He is a member of the council of the Chinese University of Hong Kong and of the board of United College. In 1972 he became President of the Hong Kong Red Cross, and in the same year was knighted for his services. He has an honorary doctorate of the University of Hong Kong. He is at present Chairman of the TVB television company (Hong Kong Television Broadcasts).

History of Hong Kong

First settlement of the Hong Kong area during the Lung Shan (also referred to as "Longshan") period (the Neolithic of northern China).	3000 B.C.
Hsia dynasty. Beginning of systematic historical writing; use of a 365-day calendar.	2523–2000 B.C. (2205–1766 B.C.)
Shang dynasty. Introduction of a written language.	2000–1122 B.C.
Chou (or "Zhou") dynasty. Development of a feudal system.	1122–249 B.C.
Ch'in ("Qin" or "Ts'in") dynasty. Trade with the great cities of the Middle East on the "silk road".	221–207 B.C.
Han dynasty. Completion of the 1800-mile-long Great Wall. China conquers South-East Asia and pushes westward to the Caspian.	206 B.C.–A.D. 220
Sung (or "Song") dynasty. Towards the end of the period the Sung are driven south by Genghis Khan's Mongols, and most of them seek refuge in the Hong Kong area. The oldest settlements on Hong Kong Island are Chek Pai Wan (Aberdeen) and Shan Kei Wan, which during the period of Mongol rule were the haunts of pirates. A people who are undoubtedly related to the aboriginal population are the Tonkas, who come closest to the description of the first inhabitants. They are incomers from what is now Vietnam, who still live on boats and in the New Territories.	A.D. 960–1279
The first Chinese settlers come to Hong Kong, including the Tang family, founders of the landholding and peasant tradition of this region.	About 1300
The Cantonese move into Hong Kong, and become known as the Puntis ("local inhabitants": Cantonese *poon tei*). They are followed by the Hakkas ("guests") and towards the end of the Ming dynasty by the Hoklos, immigrants from the northern coastal regions of China who are much given to piracy. Their language is a dialect spoken in the province of Fukien.	14th c.
First Opium War between China and Britain. Its cause is the banning by the imperial government in Peking of the profitable opium trade carried on by the British. All opium is required to be handed over to the Chinese for destruction, and British dealers and shipowners are called on to agree in writing not to import opium from India.	1840–2

History of Hong Kong

20 Jan. 1841	Convention of Chuanbi (Chuenpi). The island of Hong Kong is ceded to Britain, and the British Superintendent of Trade, Captain Charles Elliott, declares it a British colony on his own responsibility.
June 1841	Charles Elliott begins to sell land to settlers. During the year there is dissatisfaction both in China and in Britain with the Chuanbi agreement, and Elliott is replaced by Sir Henry Pottinger.
August 1841	Pottinger successively occupies Amoy, Ningpo and Shanghai.
1842	Pottinger threatens to attack Nanking, and China thereupon accepts his conditions.
29 Aug. 1842	End of the Opium War (Treaty of Nanking): Hong Kong formally ceded to Britain "in perpetuity". The towns of Amoy, Ningpo, Foochow and Shanghai are thrown open to British trade and settlement.
16 June 1843	Ratification of the Treaty of Nanking. The island officially becomes a British colony, with Sir Henry Pottinger as its first Governor.
October 1843	Supplementary agreement of Humen (Bogue). The Chinese are given free access to Hong Kong for the purposes of trade.
1851	Population of Hong Kong totalled 32,983 (of which 31,463 were Chinese).
1856–8	Second Anglo-Chinese War (wrongly called the Second Opium War), caused by the capture by the Chinese, in their search for pirates, of the "Arrow", sailing under the British flag. The war is ended by the Convention of Tientsin (Tianjin). Britain is given the right to diplomatic representation in Peking.
1860	Convention of Peking (following hostilities in 1859 and 1860). Britain acquires territory extending to Boundary Street on the Kowloon Peninsula and Stonecutters Island.
1865	Equal rights granted to the Chinese population.
1885	Construction of the Peak Tram funicular up Victoria Peak.
9 June 1898	Convention of Peking. Britain acquires the 99-year lease from China for HK $5000 (about £500) on the New Territories, "the land between", north of Boundary Street to the Shum Chun River between Deep Bay and Sha Tau Kok, along with their 236 islands.
1904	Tramway system established.
1910	Railroad line to Canton.
1911	Foundation of the University of Hong Kong.
1937–9	After the outbreak of the Sino-Japanese War some 750,000 people flee from China to Hong Kong.
1939	Hong Kong's population is now 1·6 million.

Japanese occupation of Hong Kong. (This was actually at approximately the same time as the attack on Pearl Harbor.)	8 Dec. 1941
Hong Kong surrenders to the Japanese. During the occupation Hong Kong's commercial activity comes to an almost complete halt. There are difficulties in feeding the population, and the Japanese resort to deportations. Macau takes in many refugees from Hong Kong.	24 Dec. 1941
End of the Japanese occupation. Population of Hong Kong by this time had been reduced to about 600,000.	14 Aug. 1945
Establishment of the People's Republic of China: about 750,000 refugees flood into Hong Kong. The economy stagnates because of the United Nations embargo on trade with China.	1949
Beginning of Hong Kong's industrial revolution. The foundations are laid by the developing textile industry, and this is followed by the establishment of the plastics, electronic and watchmaking industries. Hong Kong becomes an international commercial center. Social legislation and public housing lead to a steady improvement in working and living conditions.	From 1950
The Chinese government briefly relaxes frontier controls. Between 1 and 23 May more than 60,000 Chinese refugees stream into Hong Kong.	1962
In reaction to the Cultural Revolution in China the Communists in Hong Kong take advantage of conflicts over wages to promote anti-British riots.	1967
Free education is extended to all public Chinese-language elementary schools.	1971
After a period of rising prices the stock market collapses.	1973
Cantonese is given equal status with English as an official language in Hong Kong.	1974
Opening of the Mass Transit Railroad.	1980
Under new immigration laws all future illegal immigrants are to be "repatriated".	23 Oct. 1980
The British Nationality Act is passed. It came into force in January 1983 and takes from the Hong Kong Chinese their privileged status as British subjects. Since 1975 more than 100,000 Vietnamese Boat People have reached the Crown Colony.	Oct. 1981
Agreement with China that 150 "legal" immigrants a day are to be allowed to enter Hong Kong. Opening of the Ko Shan Theater.	Dec. 1982
Although protectionist measures by its main customers, especially the USA, badly affect the textile industry, an upsurge in exports reduces the deficit on trade.	1983

Dec. 1984 Hong Kong Treaty. From 1 July 1997 the Crown Colony will retain under Chinese Sovereignty its special status (free market economy, British law, English language, unrestricted freedom of travel) for a transitional period of 50 years. Hong Kong will become a "Special Administrative Region" with its own currency and laws, administered by its own elected local municipal council, but with China responsible for the former colony's security and defense.

1986 The Hong Kong government consults the administration in Peking on all major decisions. Although no one can guarantee that the Hong Kong Treaty will be binding so far as the present capitalist system is concerned, considerable foreign investment is flowing back into Hong Kong again.

Aberdeen harbour – the home of 20,000 people ▶

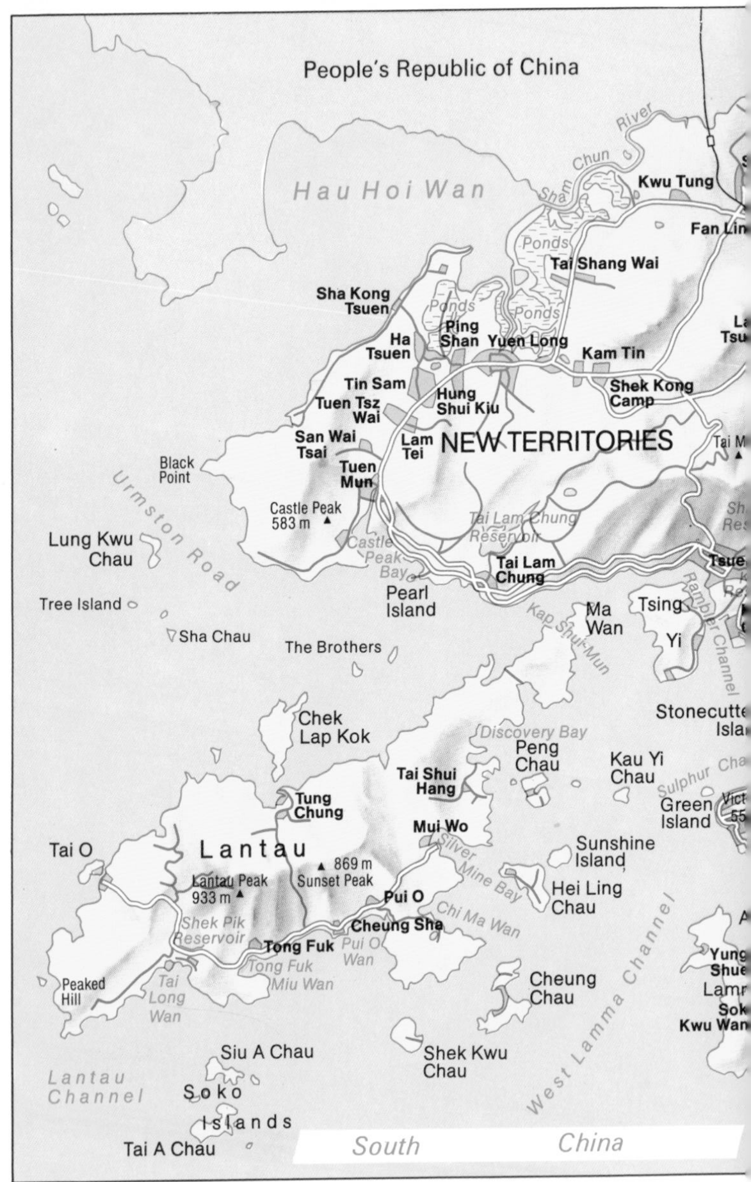
People's Republic of China
Hau Hoi Wan
Sham Chun River
Kwu Tung
Fan Lin
Ponds
Tai Shang Wai
Sha Kong Tsuen
Ponds
Ping Shan
Ponds
Ha Tsuen
Yuen Long
Kam Tin
Tin Sam
Hung Shui Kiu
Shek Kong Camp
Tuen Tsz Wai
San Wai Tsai
Lam Tei
NEW TERRITORIES
Black Point
Tuen Mun
Urmston Road
Castle Peak 583 m
Tai Lam Chung Reservoir
Lung Kwu Chau
Castle Peak Bay
Tai Lam Chung
Tree Island
Pearl Island
Kap Shui Mun
Ma Wan
Tsing Yi
Rambler Channel
Sha Chau
The Brothers
Stonecutte
Chek Lap Kok
Discovery Bay
Peng Chau
Kau Yi Chau
Tai Shui Hang
Sulphur Cha
Tung Chung
Green Island
Mui Wo
Tai O
Lantau
869 m Sunset Peak
Sunshine Island
Silver Mine Bay
Lantau Peak 933 m
Pui O
Hei Ling Chau
Chi Ma Wan
Shek Pik Reservoir
Cheung Sha
Tong Fuk
Pui O Wan
Tong Fuk Miu Wan
Peaked Hill
Tai Long Wan
Cheung Chau
West Lamma Channel
Yung Shue
Lamr
Sok Kwu Wan
Siu A Chau
Shek Kwu Chau
Lantau Channel
Soko Islands
Tai A Chau
South China

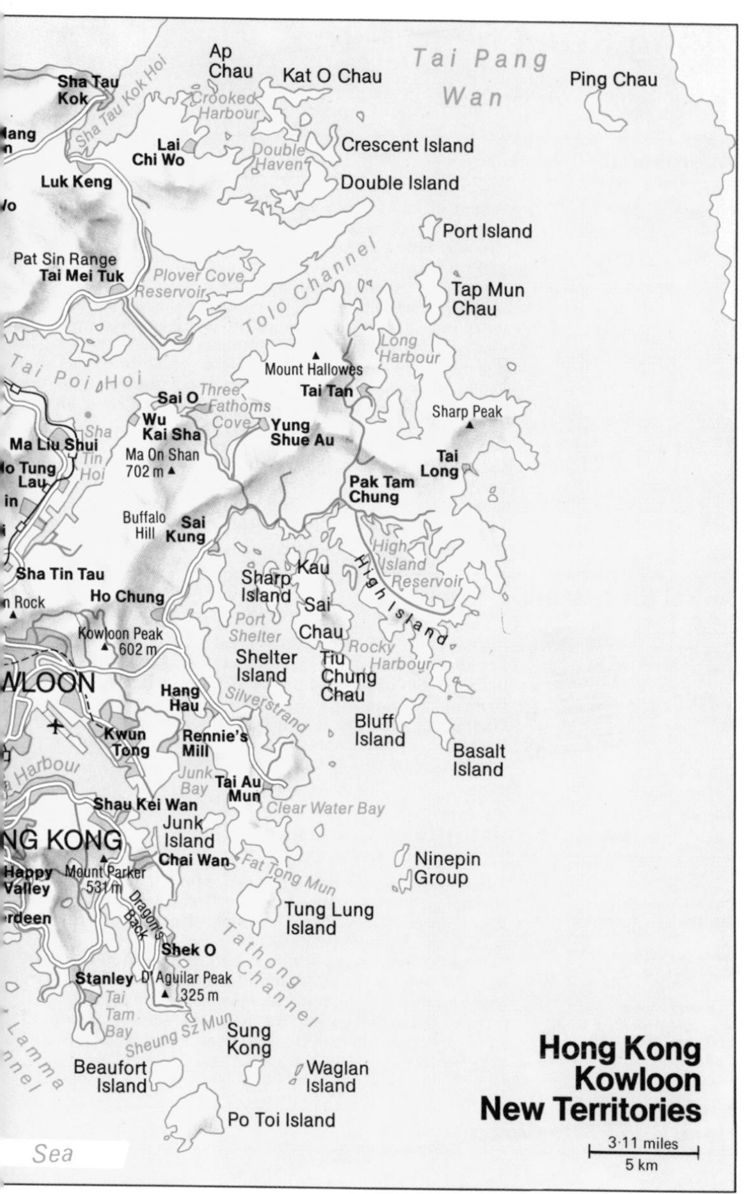
Ap Chau
Kat O Chau
Tai Pang Wan
Ping Chau
Sha Tau Kok
Sha Tau Kok Hoi
Crooked Harbour
Lai Chi Wo
Double Haven
Crescent Island
Double Island
Luk Keng
Port Island
Pat Sin Range
Tai Mei Tuk
Plover Cove Reservoir
Tolo Channel
Tap Mun Chau
Long Harbour
Tai Poi Hoi
Mount Hallowes
Tai Tan
Sai O
Three Fathoms Cove
Sharp Peak
Wu Kai Sha
Yung Shue Au
Ma Liu Shui
Sha Tin Hoi
Ma On Shan 702 m
Tai Long
Pak Tam Chung
Buffalo Hill
Sai Kung
High Island Reservoir
Kau Sai Chau
Sharp Island
High Island
Sha Tin Tau
Ho Chung
Port Shelter
Kowloon Peak 602 m
Shelter Island
Rocky Harbour
Tiu Chung Chau
Hang Hau
Silverstrand
Bluff Island
Kwun Tong
Rennie's Mill
Basalt Island
Junk Bay
Tai Au Mun
Shau Kei Wan
Clear Water Bay
Junk Island
Chai Wan
Happy Valley
Mount Parker 531 m
Fat Tong Mun
Ninepin Group
Dragon's Back
Tung Lung Island
Shek O
Tathong Channel
Stanley
D'Aguilar Peak 325 m
Tai Tam Bay
Sheung Sz Mun
Sung Kong
Beaufort Island
Waglan Island
Po Toi Island
Sea
Hong Kong
Kowloon
New Territories
3·11 miles
5 km

Hong Kong from A to Z

Aberdeen (Chek Pai Wan)

Buses
7, 72

Aberdeen, in the south-west of Hong Kong Island and named after the Earl of Aberdeen, Secretary of State for the Colonies in the mid 19th c., is probably the oldest settlement on the island, and its largest fishing "village". Today, large blocks of apartments and factories have transformed Aberdeen into a large land-based township. Some 12,000 people live on 3000 junks and sampans (small boats) in Aberdeen harbor, working mainly as fishermen or in the surrounding boatyards. A trip in a sampan will offer photographers a variety of picturesque shots, but will also reveal the prevailing poverty. (The fare should be agreed in advance: about HK $40 for a boat for half an hour.)

Aberdeen is famous for its floating restaurants; but prices tend to be high, and the standard or service has declined in recent years.

There is also a large and interesting fish market, in which the fish are sold immediately after being landed, often still alive.

Ap Lei Chau Island

Location
Just off Aberdeen

Buses
7, 72

Ap Lei Chau ("duck's tongue"), the island now linked with Aberdeen by a bridge, provides natural shelter for Aberdeen's harbor. It can be reached on foot (20 minutes), by taxi or in a sampan. The site of a big power station and the colony's boatbuilding industry, it is well worth a visit for the sake of the boatyards, where visitors can watch junks and sampans being constructed by the old traditional methods.

*Art Gallery of the Institute of Chinese Studies

Location
Chinese University, Sha Tin, New Territories

Railroad station
Sha Tin University

Opening times
Mon.–Sat. 10 a.m.–4.30 p.m., Sun. 12.30–5.30 p.m.

This fine art gallery is on the campus of the Chinese University. Divided up into four parts on different levels, its rooms open on to an inner courtyard laid out in the form of a traditional Chinese garden, using modern materials.

The gallery's extensive holdings include some 1300 exhibits from the Jen Yu Wen Collection (pictures and calligraphy by Guangdong artists from the Ming period to the present), 300 bronze seals of the Han dynasty, and collections of rubbings of stone inscriptions, mostly from the Han and Six dynasty, as well as over 400 carved jade flowers.

Hong Kong Arts Centre

Location
Queensway, Wan Chai

Opened in 1976, there is a magnificent view over the harbors from this 16-story building which, with its Shouson and Studio theaters and Recital Hall, is primarily a venue for local artistes to perform their repertoires. It is also where the Arts Festival and other international shows and events are staged.

Castle Peak (Tuen Mun)

The old Castle Peak district, renamed Tuen Mun, takes its name from the hill of that name (1913 ft/583 m), which is said to have been the scene of a number of battles, including one in 1521 when the Chinese defeated a Portuguese force which had landed here with ten ships after a two months' struggle. The most recent of the industrial establishments in this area is the sea-water desalination plant at Lok On Pai.
Residential quarters of villas set in gardens border on Tuen Mun, an expanding new satellite town with a population of over 300,000. On the slopes of Castle Peak Hill stands the Buddhist Monastery of Po Toi, with a small temple. Here, too, on Castle Peak Road, is the Dragon Garden, with reproductions of old Chinese buildings, ponds, etc. (seen only by special arrangement: information from Hong Kong Tourist Association).

Location
Western New Territories

Bus
50

Cat Street (Thieves' Market)

E

Cat Street is actually an area. The most famous street in the area is Ladder Street which leads to two rows called Upper Lascar Row; at the top is Hollywood Road. Its other name of Thieves' Market dates from the time when anyone who had had some item of property stolen could buy it back here on the following day at a very reasonable price.
The traditional street-traders and small shops have given way to new buildings and the Cat Street Market, probably the biggest market-place for Chinese antiquities outside China. The best buys are porcelain, rosewood and ebony furniture, curios and chinoiserie.

Location
Upper and Lower Lascar Row

**Causeway Bay

C

Causeway Bay, a shopping and entertainment district of many different aspects, lies to the east of the city center. Here, within the specially constructed Typhoon Shelter, are the moorings for the luxury craft of the Royal Hong Kong Yacht Club, as well as some 750 junks and sampans occupied by 2000 of Hong Kong's boat dwellers.
Just south of the Yacht Club is the World Trade Centre. The Typhoon Shelter, protected by breakwaters, is the third of Hong Kong's typhoon havens (the others being the harbors of Aberdeen and Yau Ma Tei – see entries). With the opening of the Cross-Harbour Tunnel the quarter has developed into even more of a district for restaurants and shopping. In the months of April to October, from about 8 in the evening, visitors can enjoy a succulent meal of fish on one of the sampans which are rowed around the harbor by women. The boats can be hired by the hour, but it is essential to agree a price in advance (about

Buses
5B, 25

Bird's eye view of Cheung Chau Island

HK $ 70 an hour). There are no regular menus: you make up your own meal by buying shrimps, crayfish, shellfish, etc., and drinks from the kitchen and bar sampans which come alongside. There are also boats carrying Chinese musicians who, for a fee, will provide a musical accompaniment to your meal.

Opposite the Typhoon Shelter are the 950-roomed Excelsior Hotel, with an air-conditioned shopping arcade and the Tung Yee Village (small shops selling craft articles and Chinese medicines), together with various department stores, countless small shops and the famous Food Street with its numerous restaurants – where one can try a Chinese-style breakfast in the early morning.

*Cheung Chau Island

Ferries
From Outlying Districts Ferry Pier, Connaught Road, Hong Kong;
to Cheung Chau
6.25 a.m.–11 p.m.;
from Cheung Chau
5.45 a.m.–10.30 p.m.

Cheung Chau is a small island about 7½ miles/12 km west of Hong Kong. The population of almost 30,000 has no traffic problems: there are no cars on the island, and people get about on foot.

Pak Tai Temple

The bay on the west side of the island provides an anchorage for hundreds of fishermen's junks; on the other side lies the Tung Wan beach with many restaurants; and on the hill between the two bays is the Pak Tai Temple, built in 1783 and most recently renovated in 1903. This Taoist temple, in a style typical of the period, contains a sword of the Sung period (920–1279) which was recovered from the sea just off the coast and presented to the god Pi Tai, to whom the temple is dedicated.

Po Chai Cave
At the south-west tip of the island, near Sai Wan, is a temple of Tin Hau, Queen of Heaven and patron saint of seafarers, and the cave where the notorious pirate Po Chai once had his lair. From here, in the early 18th c., he preyed on shipping in the South China Sea with a fleet of 300 junks until the coming of the British put an end to his activities.

Prehistoric rock engravings
At the height of some 13 ft/4 m above the road to the right of Tung Wan beach are a number of small prehistoric rock-engravings. They are, however, difficult to find.
This is where the colorful Bun Festival is held in April/May. Surfboards for Tung Wan and Kwun Yum Wan beaches can be hired from Kent's Windsurfing Centre.

Ching Chuen Koong Temple

Location
Castle Peak Road, near Castle Peak Hospital

Buses
2 to Jordan Road, then 50

The Taoist "Temple of the Green Pirates" contains lanterns over 200 years old, a jade seal, more than a thousand years old, and several temple watchman statues, carved in Peking and dating from 300 years ago. The principal temple in this handsome complex, built in 1959, is dedicated to Lui Tung-pin (Liu Shui in Cantonese), one of the Eight Immortals of Taoism, who is usually depicted with a magical sword which enables him to make himself invisible and to conceal himself in the sky. The other Immortals are Han Hsiang Tzu, Lau Tsai-Ho, Chung-Li Chuan, Chang Kuo, Ho Hsien Ku, Li Tieh-Kwai and Tsao Kuo-Chin.
Two of the buildings in the complex contains thousands of tablets commemorating ancestors, some of them reserved for people who are still alive. On the temple walls are inscribed Taoist texts.

*City Hall F/G

Location
Edinburgh Place, 2 min. from Star Ferry Pier

Opening times
9 a.m.–midnight

Hong Kong's first town hall, built in 1869, was pulled down in 1933 under a land reclamation scheme. The new City Hall was built on a site reclaimed from the sea and opened to the public in 1962. It is the seat of the municipal administration and at the same time a cultural center for the people of Hong Kong.
The complex includes a concert hall seating 1500, a theater seating 460, one large and several smaller exhibition rooms, rooms for musical recitals, movie shows and lectures, art galleries, restaurants and a library.
The programme of entertainments offered in the City Hall covers a very wide range – concerts of Western classical music by the Hong Kong Philharmonic and leading international orchestras, Chinese classical music and Chinese operas; performances of ballet and drama; a variety of exhibitions (including exhibitions of Chinese folk art); movies from many different countries, etc.

Concert hall in the City Hall, Hong Kong's cultural center

On the 10th and 11th floors, in the High Block, is the Hong Kong Museum of Art (see entry), containing a collection of Chinese antiquities (ceramics, lacquerware, jade, cloisonné, paper-cuts, embroidery), 17th–19th c. paintings and calligraphy, and over 1000 works of art by artists from Hong Kong and neighboring countries.

Coliseum

Location
Salisbury Road
Tsim Sha Tsui
East Kowloon

This impressive, pyramid-shaped building was completed in April 1983. The covered arena seats 12,500, and is used for ballet, ice shows and the Hong Kong Philharmonic's pop classic concerts, as well as sporting events.

Flagstaff House Museum of Tea

Location
Victoria Barracks (entrance on Cotton Tree Drive)

Opening times
Daily (except Wed.)
10 a.m.–5 p.m.

The Flagstaff House Museum of Tea, opened in January 1984, occupies the oldest Western-style building still standing in Hong Kong. Once the home of the Commander of the Armed Forces, its architecture is typical of Hong Kong in the mid 19th c.
The collection, which includes a bequest from Dr K. S. Lo, is centered on tea-sets from the time of the Feuding Kingdoms up to the present. The Yi Xing teaware is particularly worth seeing.

*Fung Ping Shan Museum

K

This museum, founded in 1953 within the University of Hong Kong on the initiative of Professor F. S. Drake, specializes in Chinese ceramics and bronzes.
The collection of bronzes is divided into three groups: ritual vessels of the Shang and Chou dynasties, decorative mirrors from the Warrior period to the T'ang dynasty, and 966 Nestorian crosses of the Yuan dynasty – the largest collection of its kind in the world. The collection of ceramics includes painted pottery of the 3rd millennium B.C., work of the Han and T'ang dynasties and the magnificent and world-famed "blue-and-white" porcelain of the Ming and Ch'ing dynasties, as well as more recent works by Jingdezhen and Shiwan potters.
The Museum also has paintings from the Ming and Ch'ing dynasties, and sculptures in stone, jade, lacquer and bamboo.

Location
94 Bonham Road,
University of Hong Kong

Buses
3, 23, 103

Opening times
Daily (except Sun.)
9.30 a.m.–6 p.m.

Conducted tours
In English

Happy Valley

This sprawling urban district in the interior of the island, south of Causeway Bay, is the second oldest British settlement in Hong Kong. Its big sports complexes include a racetrack, and the Queen Elizabeth Stadium near by often stages concerts as well. An interesting insight into local history is provided by the four cemeteries – Persian, Catholic, Muslim and Colonial – in the street behind the Royal Hong Kong Jockey Club.

Herbarium

The Hong Kong Herbarium, founded in 1878, is full of interest for botanists and plant-lovers. It contains more than 33,000 different plant specimens representative of Hong Kong flora, identified by their Latin, English, and Chinese names.
The Herbarium is open Monday to Friday 10 a.m.–noon and 2–4 p.m., Saturdays 9.30–11 a.m.; closed on Sunday. Admission is free.

Location
New World Centre Office Building, Tsim Sha Tsui.
Administered by: Agriculture and Fisheries Department, 393 Canton Road, Kowloon

Hong Kong and Shanghai Bank

The Hong Kong and Shanghai Bank's new headquarters, the work of British architect Norman Forster, were opened in April 1986, when this was accounted the most expensive single building in the world. This silver-grey, hi-tech steel, glass and aluminum office building is a 52-story skyscraper, almost 590 ft/179 m high, housing 3500 employees. The atrium has a remarkable lighting system. A computer-operated mirror on the south façade reflects the sunlight on to a further mirror over the atrium, and 120 built-in lasers then transfer the daylight to the hall. Further refinements are the dining-room in the penthouse and a helicopter pad on the roof. Stitt and Stephen, the two bronze lions that guard the new building's main entrance, as for 50 years they guarded the old, have recently been incorporated into the design on the back of the Hong Kong dollar.

Jade Market

Location
Yaumati,
Kowloon
Kausu Street and
Reclamation Street
Daily 10 a.m.–4 p.m.

The pieces for sale in Hong Kong's jade market, by far the biggest in the world, are nowadays almost always reproductions. There are basically three qualities of raw jade, with the top-quality stone resembling emeralds of exceptional purity and color, then there is the gemstone jade found in most jewelers' shops, and finally the ordinary jade sold on the street, where the "fingerjade" pieces are also very popular. These symbolic fruits and animal figures were originally put in graves to ward off the decay of mortality (see Practical Information – Antiques).

Jervois Street

E

Between the Macau Ferry Terminal and Queen's Road is Jervois Street, famous for its shops which specialize in the selling of snakes. Every year when the colder weather sets in, the Jervois Street dealers offer for sale huge numbers of snakes of all sizes and species, which form a favourite Chinese food supply during the winter. The snakes are used to make a soup which – so the Chinese maintain – warms the body from within and prevents the winter cold from entering their limbs.
No fewer than 50,000 cobras alone are made into soup every year. Since snake meat has no taste chicken stock is added, and this gives the soup its flavour.

*Kam Tin Village

Location
New Territories

Buses
51 from Tai Kok Tsui,
74 from Yuen Long

The 500-year-old village of Kat Hing Wai (better known as Kam Tin), surrounded by walls and a moat, lies in the Kam Tin district in the Western New Territories. A charge is made for admission to the village; the main street is lined on both sides by shops and stalls selling handmade goods and souvenirs; and the old people of the village allow themselves to be photographed in return for suitable payment.
The village, with a remarkable wrought-iron gate at the entrance, is very typical of the Chinese building style of the period. Much of it is still original, but here and there the old houses have been replaced by newer ones. The village is laid out on a geometric plan, with narrow lanes leading off the main street and giving access to the individual houses.
All the inhabitants of the village belong to the Tang clan. It is now mostly occupied by older people: the youinger poeple work in the city, but when they reach the age of retirement they come back to the village, even if they have spent their working life overseas.
Near by is another walled village, Wing Lung Wai, which was also established by a member of the Tang clan 500 years ago. In the north-eastern district of Fanling is Lung Yeuk Tan, with a group of 11 villages, five of them walled. Sun Wai, the best preserved of these villages, was established some 400 years ago. Tsang Tai Uk (formerly known as Sha Ha Wei), which dates from the time of the Ch'ing dynasty, lies south of the town of Sha Tin and is inhabited by the Hakka people; the women wear wide-brimmed straw hats with a black curtain-like fringe.

Ko Shan Theatre

Opened in 1983, the Ko Shan Theatre is Hong Kong's first open-air theater. It has 2000 seats under cover and 1500 in the open, and puts on Chinese opera and pop, variety and movie shows.

Location
Kowloon

Ladder Street

Ladder Street cuts across Hollywood Road at the Man Mo Temple. It is a series of steep flights of steps running down to Upper and Lower Lascar Rows (see "Cat Street" entry) past the shops of Chinese craftsmen.

Lai Chi Kok Amusement Park

If you are interested in Cantonese operas this amusement park in north-western Kowloon is the place to visit. The performances which last almost three hours and attract enthusiastic audiences, take place almost ever day at about 8 p.m. Other attractions offered to its mostly working-class visitors include sports facilities, games of chance and all kinds of popular entertainment. Here, too, there are reproductions of the old Chung Chu Palace in Peking and the Siu Sai Wu Lake (Canton).

Location
Kwoloon

Buses
6, 6A

Opening times
11 a.m.–11 p.m.

Admission charge

Ladder Street

Outside the park is the enormous Mei Foo Su Chuen condominium complex, and the Choy Lee shipyard, where visitors can see junks being built.
In the amusement park, but operated separately, is the Sung Dynasty Village (see entry), which reproduces in detail life in a typical village curing the Sung dynasty (960–1279), the most fascinating period in China's history.

Lamma Island

Ferries
From Outlying Islands District Pier, Connaught Road, Hong Kong

Only 40 minutes by ferry from Hong Kong, traffic-free Lamma Island (pop. 8500) is pleasantly rural and becoming a favorite spot for weekenders. As in many maritime communities, the main village, Yung Shue Wan, has a Tin Hau temple (dating from the Sung dynasty). The festival of this patron saint of seafarers takes place in late March/early April every year on the island.
The island's highest point is Mount Stenhouse (1165 ft/ 353 m). There are also fine sandy beaches (with toilets, etc.) at Hung Shing Ye, Lo So Shing and Mo Tat Wan, and plenty of open-air harborside restaurants.

**Lantau Island

Ferries
From Outlying Districts Ferry Pier, Connaught Road, Hong Kong:
to Silvermine Bay, 7 a.m.–11.25 p.m.;
from Silvermine Bay, 6.15 a.m.–10 p.m.;
to Tai O, 9.30 a.m.–9.10 p.m.;
from Tai O, 6.10 a.m.–6.30 p.m.

Accommodation
Po Lin Monastery, tel. 5-985426; Trappist Haven (apply Grand Master, P.O. Box 5, Peng Chau, Hong Kong).

Lantau Island ("Big Island Mountain") lies to the west of Hong Kong and is by far the Crown Colony's biggest island, but has a population of only 16,000, despite, at 55 square miles/ 142 sq km, being twice the size of Hong Kong. Its biggest settlement is Tai O (pop. 6600), with houses built on piles over the river which flows through the town.
The best known of its many temples and Buddhist monasteries is dedicated to Kwan Ti, the god of war.

Po Lin Monastery
From Silvermine Bay a No. 2 bus goes to this "Monastery of the Precious Lotus" at a height of 2625 ft/800 m near Ngong Ping on the slopes of Lantau Peak 3079 ft/933 m. The monastery was founded in 1921, and later two additional two-story temples were built. The main temple contains three Buddha statues. Accommodation for visitors is provided on hard plank beds, in separate buildings for men and women, with vegetarian meals. It is well worth rising early to climb Lantau Peak, under the guidance of a monk, to see the magnificent sunrise.
Below the monastery, to the south, are the tea plantations on the Ngong Ping plateau, where there is accommodation for visitors in small air-conditioned bungalows.

Shek Pik Reservoir
This reservoir, from which water is conveyed under ground to Cheung Chau and Hong Kong, lies amid scenery of breath-taking beauty to the west of Pui O and Cheung Sha beaches (north of the Tai O road). There is a magnificent walk around the lake. A new maximum security prison is under construction at Shek Pik; and a closed camp for refugees has been constructed at Chi Ma Wan on Lantau Island.

In Po Lin Monastery, Lantau

On a Lantau tea plantation

Tung Chung Fort
There is also a bus service to Tung Chung, in the north-west of the island, where the population is mainly engaged in farming. An interesting feature here is the fort, built by the Chinese in 1817 as a defense against the advancing Europeans.

Trappist Haven
Also of interest, in the north-east of the island, is the Trappist Haven of Our Lady of Liesse, established in 1956 by monks fleeing from the new régime in Peking. The Trappists, who have taken a vow of silence, run a dairy farm which sells its produce to the city. Here, too, there are accommodations for visitors (advance booking advisable). The monastery can be reached either on foot from Silvermine Bay or by taking a ferry to the island of Peng Chau and crossing from there to Lantau on a sampan which puts in below the monastery.
Silvermine Bay (Mui Wo – pop. 4000) has a fine sandy beach, with water-sports facilities, and its old silver-mine and Man Mo Temple are worth visiting.
The exclusive Sea Ranch Club, which can only be reached by helicopter or de luxe ferry, has an excellent cuisine (specialities), tennis-courts and Hong Kong's biggest private swimming-pool.

**Lau Fau Shan

Location
Western New Territories

Lau Fau Shan, a small fishing village on Deep Bay (Western New Territories), is famous for its oysters, which have been

Oyster culture, Lau Fau Shan

cultivated here for several hundred years. Some 100 tons of oysters are harvested here every year, and almost the whole of the village is built on oyster-shells, which are regularly deposited in the sea in the effort to reclaim additional land.
In the narrow main streets a variety of fish and seafood, vegetables and meat are offered for sale, and there are small restaurants which serve fresh fish bought to order from the neighboring stalls. Alternatively visitors can buy their own food and have it cooked in one of the restaurants.
Here, too, there is a 1500-year-old temple founded by the legendary monk Pui To, who is said to have landed on this coast in a wooden tub.

Buses
50 from Jordan Road to Yuen Long, then 55

**Lei Cheng Uk Tomb

The vaulted tomb, Hong Kong's oldest historical monument, dates from the Late Han dynasty (206 B.C.–A.D. 221) which makes it about 1900 years old. It was discovered in 1955 during excavations for a new housing estate.
Built in brick on a uniform plan, the tomb has four chambers around a central arched vault. The archeologists who excavated the site found 58 pottery and bronze articles, now displayed in the small site museum. The tomb is now under the guardianship of the Museum of History (see entry) and is open to the public (admission charge; photography not permitted).
Visitors to the tomb can hardly help seeing something of the life of the huge housing estate which surrounds it. In this area about 100,000 people live in modern, but terribly overcrowded, housing conditions.

Location
41 Tonkin Street
Shamshuipo,
Kowloon

Buses
2, 6

Opening times
Daily 10 a.m.–1 p.m., and 2–6 p.m., Sun. and public holidays 1–6 p.m.

Closed Tues.

Admission charge

*Lit Shing Kung Temple

E

This Taoist temple, in the same building as the Man Mo Temple (see entry), is dedicated to several divinities – Kuan Ying (goddess of mercy), Ran Tung (god of light), Wong Tai Sin (he who hears all prayers), Kuan Ti (the god Mo) and many more. Taoism came under some degree of Buddhist influence, taking over for example the Buddhist deities Kuan Yin and Ran Tung.

Location
124 Hollywood Road,
Hong Kong

Opening times
Daily

**Lok Ma Chau

At Lok Ma Chau police station there is an observation terrace which affords an extensive view of Chinese territory. In the plain below can be seen an expanse of rice-fields and farmhouses, traversed by the frontier river Sham Chun, flowing some distance away. In front of the next range of hills is the first sizeable town in the People's Republic of China.
The people of Lok Ma Chau display the usual Chinese business enterprise – hiring out binoculars, selling souvenirs and (particularly the older inhabitants) sitting, for a fee, for amateur photographers.

Location
On Chinese frontier

Buses
50 from Jordan Road to Yuen Long, then 76 or 77

Lei Cheng Uk Tomb

Interior of the Lei Chen Uk Tomb (Han dynasty)

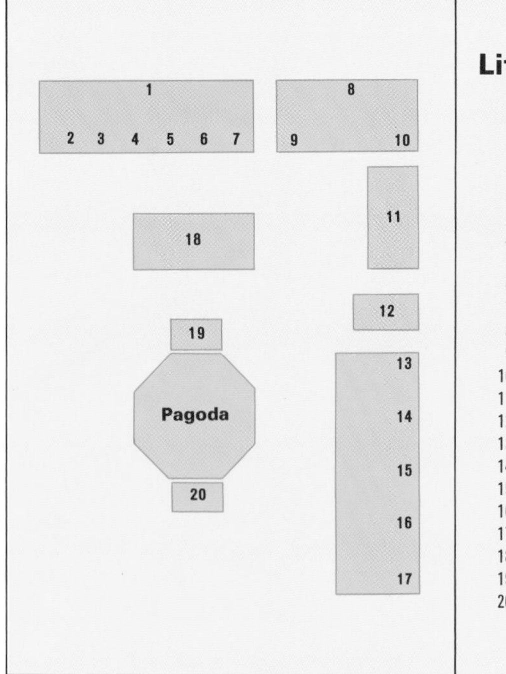

Lit Shing Kung Temple

1 God of Light
2 God of Wealth
3 Wong Tai Sin
4 Kuan Ti
5 God of Learning
6 God of Wealth
7 God of Study
8 Bau Kung
9 Monkey God
10 Kwan Kung
11 Sixty Year Gods
12 Fairy
13 Tin Hau
14 Pi Tai
15 Dragon Mother
16 God of Fire
17 Wah Tin
18 Goddess of Mercy
19 Protector of the Law
20 Goddess of Mercy

View of the People's Republic of China from Lok Ma Chau

Altar in Man Mo Temple

**Man Mo Temple E

Location
124 Hollywood Road, Hong Kong

Opening times
Daily

The Man Mo Temple, built by Taoists in 1848 and last renovated in 1894, is one of the largest and best-known temples on the island of Hong Kong. It is dedicated to two gods, Man and Mo.

Man, one of the gods of literature, was born in A.D. 287 as Cheung Ah Tse. He is particularly revered by officials and statesmen.

Mo, now worshipped as a war god, was born in A.D. 160 under the name of Kwan Yue; he is also known as Kuan Ti or Kuan Kung. He fought against injustice and oppression, and was killed in 219 after being captured by his enemies. In 1594, under the Ming dynasty, the Emperor Wan Li granted him the style of "Great, Venerable and Loyal Ti, Assistant of Heaven and Protector of the Empire". He is the tutelary god of the Hong Kong police.

Both of these gods were emperors in the early period of China, and under their rule the country enjoyed a period of peace and prosperity.

*Museum of Art F/G

Location
City Hall High Block
Floors 10/11
Hong Kong

The Hong Kong Museum of Art is housed on the 10th and 11th floors of the City Hall (see entry), 2 minutes' walk from the Star Ferry Pier. Its principal attraction is its collection of Chinese art and antiquities. The exhibits include ceramics, bronzes,

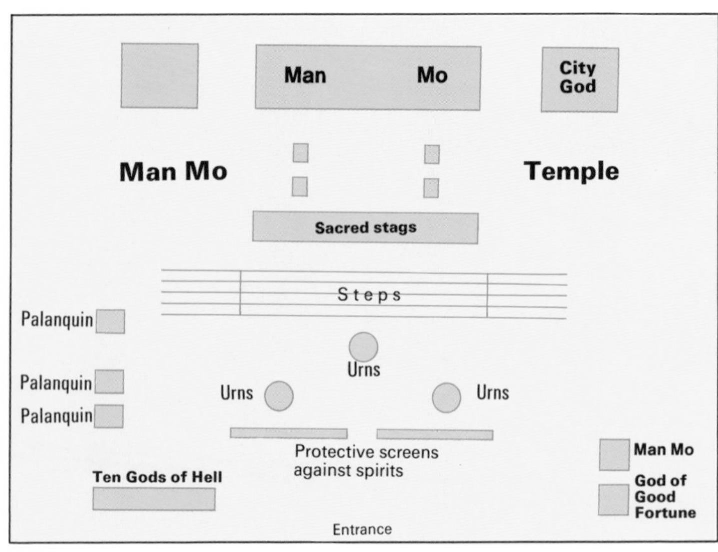

Hong Kong Museum of Art

calligraphy, jade, paintings, paper-cuts and lacquerware; and the museum's collection of over 1000 pictures, prints, drawings and lithographs gives an excellent view of 18th and 19th c. art. There are also some 700 contemporary works of art by artists from Hong Kong and neighboring countries. There are conducted tours in English and Chinese.

Opening times
Mon.–Wed., Fri. and Sat.
10 a.m.–6 p.m.
Sun. and public holidays
1–6 p.m.

Closed Thurs.

Museum of Chinese Cultural Relics

This museum, opened in 1984, houses a permanent exhibition of cultural treasures from China. Archeological finds date from as early as prehistory and testify to the high level of technique and craftsmanship achieved in earlier epochs. The museum is open daily 10 a.m. to 6 p.m. and there is a charge for admission.

Location
Causeway Centre
1st floor
28 Harbour Road
Wan Chai

*Museum of History

This museum was founded by the Urban Council in 1975, and is officially responsible for all excavation carried out in Hong Kong. Its collection centers on history, archeology and ethnography. Photographs of the 19th and 20th c. illustrate the development of the colony, while the earlier phases of the region's history are documented by archeological material. The ethnographical department is concerned with arts and crafts, religious beliefs, agriculture and architecture.
The museum is closed on Fridays.

Location
Kowloon Park
Haiphong Road
Tsimshatsui
Kowloon

Opening times
Mon.–Thurs., Sat. 10 a.m.–6 p.m. Sun. and public holidays 1–6 p.m.

Nathan Road

F/G/L/R/V/W/Z

Nathan Road – Kowloon's "Golden Mile" – runs north in a dead straight line through Kowloon from the new Harbour City

NARDIN
FINE WATCHES
LTD.
エンプレース
帝后華
EMPRESS
BAR
家酒
AH CHUK TAILOR
Russian
2 DRAGONS
BAR
CUPIDS BAR
2 DRAGONS
BAR
BAR

complex to Boundary Street and the New Territories, crossing the shopping streets of Mong Kok, with its bird market tucked away in Hong Lok Street and selling all kinds of exotic birds, such as parrots, cockatoos, etc.
The bustling Golden Mile, with its constant stream of traffic, including the MTR, is lined on both sides with hotels, restaurants, department stores, smaller shops, movie theaters, bars, night-clubs, etc., in fact, an abundance of wares and entertainment of all kinds.
About a quarter of a mile from the harbor, on the west side of Nathan Road, lies Kowloon Park, containing a large new Islamic Center and mosque, and the Museum of History (see entry).

*Night Market

R/V

During the day Temple Street, which runs north from Jordan Road on a line roughly parallel with Nathan Road (see preceding entry), is a perfectly normal street in western Kowloon, but in the evening, like the Macau Ferry Wharf, it becomes a "Poor Man's Night-club" (see entry). Street traders offer an endless variety of wares, and steam-kitchens serve simple but succulent dishes. Visitors should try some of this fare – remember, any food that is boiled is likely to be hygienically safe.

Location
Temple Street, Kowloon

Opening times
Daily 8 p.m. to midnight

**Ocean Park

Ocean Park, on 170 acres of land and Asia's largest oceanarium, lies on the Shum Shui peninsula, west of Deep Water Bay and east of Aberdeen (see entry). The park is on two levels, linked by a cableway 1500 yd/1·4 km long. On the lower level, the Lowland site, are a park, a playground, water-gardens, plants from all over the world, exotic birds, and animals from many countries. Here, too, there are various cultural events and other attractions.
From the lower level it is a 7-minute trip by cable car (with fine views of the South China Sea and the numerous offshore islands) to the upper level, the Headland site, with the Ocean Theatre, in which dolphins, a killer whale and seals are put through their paces before anything up to 4000 spectators. To the left of this is Wave Cove, an artificially constructed rocky creek with machine-generated waves which affords a naturalistic setting for seals and sealions, penguins and dolphins. From the top there is a magnificent view of the teeming junks in Aberdeen harbor.
The principal attraction, however, is the Atoll Reef near the cableway station, a deep-sea aquarium (said to be the world's biggest) with more than 30,000 fish, including sharks and rays. Thick glass panels enable visitors to watch the fish in the aquarium and observe the beauty of the corals on three different levels, going down to 20 ft/6 m below the surface.
Further redevelopments in 1982–3 feature a second entrance to the Park from Thai Shue Wan Bay, water recreational area, more

Location
Ocean Park Road,
Hong Kong

Buses
4, 48, 71A, 72, 73

Opening times
Mon.–Sat. 10 a.m.–6 p.m.
Sun. and public holidays
9 a.m.–6 p.m.

Admission charge
c. HK $70

◀ *Nathan Road, the pulsating centre of Kowloon*

Ocean Park: feeding the dolphins

New World Centre

shops, restaurants and a children's "adventure world", and a roller coaster.
There is an admission charge for entry to Ocean Park (either to the whole area or to the lower level alone).
The 71A bus runs direct from the Central Bus Terminal in Hong Kong to Ocean Park on Sundays and public holidays. The other lines stop in Wong Chuk Hang Road, opposite the Ocean Park car park.

*Ocean Terminal

Y

The Ocean Terminal, at the southern tip of Kowloon, is both a landing-place for cruise ship passengers and a shopping center, with more than 100 shops on two levels. It is now linked with the still larger Ocean Centre, opened in 1978, which also contains streets of shops. Together they form a huge shopping complex, from the roof of which there are extensive views of the port installations and the island of Hong Kong.
Opposite the Sheraton Hotel is the New World Centre, which is almost as large and is also stocked with an abundance of wares to satisfy the most enthusiastic shopper.
On the top floor is a huge restaurant with seating for no fewer than 6000 people.

Location
Tsim Sha Tsui, Kowloon

Pao Sui Loon Galleries

This gallery, which is on the 4th and 5th floors of the Hong Kong Arts Centre, does not have a permanent exhibition, but hosts big local and international exhibitions throughout the year, with the emphasis on contemporary art.

Location
Harbour Road, Wan Chai

Opening times
Daily 10 a.m.–8 p.m.

Peng Chau Island

Peng Chau, lying off the north-east coast of the island of Lantau (see entry), has a population of 10,000. There are no cars on the island. The inhabitants live mainly by fishing and farming.
There is a temple, built in 1792, dedicated to the goddess Tin Hau.
It is worth paying a visit to the porcelain workshop of Wah Lee to watch him at his skilled and intricate work.

Ferries
From Outlying Districts Ferry Pier, Connaught Road, Hong Kong:
to Peng Chau, 7 a.m.–11.15 p.m.;
from Peng Chau, 6.35 a.m.–10.20 p.m.

Ping Shan Village

The ancient little village of Ping Shan, north-west of Yuen Long (New Territories), has a 500-year-old pagoda, built by the Tang clan who live in the village. The pagoda originally had five stories , but the top two stories were torn off by a typhoon in 1954.

Location
Western New Territories

The Poor Man's Night-club

**Poor Man's Night-club

E

Location
Macau Ferry Pier,
Connaught Road,
Hong Kong

Buses 1, 2

Opening times
Daily 8 p.m.–midnight

Every evening about 8 the car park at the Macau Ferry Pier becomes a busy street market, known as the Poor Man's Night-club. Hundreds of stalls display a great variety of wares, including tasty dishes of seafood (which tourists need have no hesitation in sampling). Chinese street musicians and actors add to the liveliness of the scene – making no charge for their performances but nevertheless expecting a small contribution from the onlookers.

*Repulse Bay

Buses
6, 260

Repulse Bay is Hong Kong's most popular beach, often having more than 200,000 visitors at weekends. The Repulse Bay Hotel is one of the few relics of the early colonial period.
There is a huge statue of Tin Hau, queen of heaven and patroness of seafarers and fishermen, together with a number of other statues of divinities, of no great artistic quality.

Sai Kung Village

Location
Eastern New Territories

Sai Kung is a little market center and fishing port in a beautiful setting in the Eastern New Territories. The Sai Kung Country Park makes a welcome change from the hectic big-city life of

Kowloon and Victoria, with its lakes, woodland, hilltop views and many beautiful walks and drives.
South of Sai Kung is the yachting harbor of Hebe Haven.
To reach the beaches of Hap Mun, Kiu Tsin and Pak Sha Chan, on islands lying just offshore, get off the bus about $1\frac{1}{4}$ miles/ 2 km before Sai Kung and take the little ferry across to the islands.

Buses
5 or 9 from Star Ferry Pier, Kowloon;
92 from Choi Hung

Sha Tin

Sha Tin is the largest of the new towns around Hong Kong and is expected to have a population approaching 850,000 by the mid 1990s. In this satellite town are the Chinese University, the Art Gallery of the Institute of Chinese Studies (see entry) and the Temple of 10,000 Buddhas (see entry). Here, too, in 1978 the Royal Hong Kong Jockey Club opened a second race-course, on which there are races every weekend, and which has Penfold Park in its center. (Their first racetrack is in Happy Valley, see entry.) South of Sha Tin towers the famous Amah Rock which looks like a woman with a child on her back.

Location
Eastern New Territories

Rail service
From Hung Hom, Kowloon

Shenzhen (Kwangtung, People's Republic of China)

Just over the border the People's Republic of China has set up the Shenzhen "Special Economic Zone" (including a big amusement park) which can be visited with a special 3-day

Location
Kwangtung, People's Republic of China

Repulse Bay: a beautiful bay with a magnificent backdrop

Rail service
From Hung Hom, Kowloon, via Lo Wu

visa. The usual way to get there is by rail, crossing the frontier at Lo Wu. (Bookings and information from travel agents in Hong Kong.)

Space Museum

Location
Salisbury Road, Kowloon

Opening times
Space Theatre
Mon., Wed.–Sat., English/Chinese conducted tours 2.30, 4, 5.30, 7.30, 9 p.m.; Sun. also 11 a.m., 12.30 p.m.
Exhibition halls
Daily (except Thurs.) 10.30 a.m./2–10 p.m.

Opened in 1980, the Space Museum forms part of one of the world's biggest planetariums. Exhibits in its main exhibition hall include the Aurora 7 space capsule. The Hall of Solar Sciences has an automatic solar telescope, audio-visual displays, micro-computers, etc.

During the shows in the Space Theatre over 9000 star configurations can be projected on to the dome of the planetarium, measuring 76 ft/23 m in diameter and affording a 360° panorama. The special effects are intensified by over 300 projectors and a computerized audio-visual system. There is an admission charge.

Stanley (peninsula)

Sited on this peninsula in the south-west of Hong Kong Island is the colony's main prison, which the Japanese occupation forces also used as a prison camp to intern the British during the Second World War. The former fishing village of Stanley is now a residential town and has a very popular market (clothes are a particular bargain) and an interesting 1767 Tin Hau Temple. There is swimming off the narrow beach on Stanley Bay, and it is well worth taking a walk to the Tai Tam Reservoir in the north of the peninsula.

**Sung Dynasty Village

Location
Lai Chi Kok Amusement Park, Kowloon

Bus
6A

This small-scale reproduction of a village of the Sung period (A.D. 960–1279), in north-western Kowloon, took four years to complete. Along the banks of an artificially created river stand a series of pavilions built of sprucewood. "Villagers" in period costume demonstrate the processes of manufacture of sweetmeats and noodles, and visitors are tempted into a herb shop, a tavern, a shop selling fans, various traditional craft workshops, and the "House of the Rich Man", with its solid furniture, lacquer and bronze. There is also a waxworks with figures spanning 5000 years of history (including Emperor Ping, the last of the Sung dynasty and the only emperor to have set foot in Hong Kong, Chairman Mao and Chiang Kaishek), and a restaurant which serves food prepared from old Sung recipes. From time to time there are special events – wedding ceremonies, dances, kung fu displays, performances by trained monkeys, court parades, etc.

There are three types of admission ticket, in different price ranges. The most expensive includes the bus trip, a Sung dynasty lunch and vouchers for certain goods on sale in the village; in the second category the Sung meal is replaced by a snack; and the cheapest ticket covers only a sightseeing visit on Saturdays, Sundays, and public holidays.

The Sung Dynasty Village: old China in miniature

Tai Lam Chung Reservoir

The Tai Lam Chung Reservoir, lying between Tsuen Wan (an industrial city with some 1,000,000 inhabitants and a recently opened new City Hall) and Tuen Mun (with huge new housing developments), is Hong Kong's largest reservoir. Here the water which flows down from the mountains is collected, purified and distributed to the consumers in the surrounding area. The reservoir is beautifully situated and surrounded by attractive footpaths.

Location
Western New Territories

Tai Mo Shan

Tai Mo Shan is the highest point in the colony (3140 ft/957 m). It is best reached by taxi. On the summit is a weather station belonging to the Royal Observatory, which can be visited by prior appointment. In clear weather there is a good view of the Chinese mainland from here.

Location
New Territories

Bus
51 from Tai Kok Tsui

*Tai Po

This town, once a pirates' lair and now an important market center with a projected population of over 250,000, and an Industrial Estate which is semi-constructed, lies in Tolo

Location
Northern New Territories

瑞氣
TIGER BALM

Harbour, an inlet in the Northern New Territories. 1¼ miles/2 km south is a harbor from which there are ferry services to the island of Tap Mun (either a direct crossing or a longer trip calling in at a number of small places on the coast; time between 75 and 150 minutes.
Tap Mun has a fishing harbor, a temple and a typical street of shops offering a variety of wares. It offers fine views of the South China Sea and the Chinese coast across Mirs Bay.

Bus
70 from Jordan Road

Rail service
From Hung Hom

**Temple of 10,000 Buddhas

The Temple of 10,000 Buddhas (the 10,000 is now more like 12,800), situated at an altitude of some 1050 ft/320 m, can be reached only by climbing a steep flight of steps: a strenuous climb which should be attempted in summer only by those who are fully fit.
The temple complex is on two levels – the principal temple on the lower level and the second temple, consisting of four separate structures, on the upper. The principal temple, built in 1950, is dedicated to Kuan Yin, and has in the forecourt a nine-story pagoda with figures of the Buddha in different postures.
The temple farthest to the right on the upper level contains the body of the founder, a monk named Yuet Kai, who came to Hong Kong after the Second World War and built the temple complex with financial help from local Buddhists. Yuet Kai died in 1965 at the age of 87. His embalmed body was subsequently lacquered and gilded, and on 26 May 1966 (Buddha's birthday) it was placed, in the seated Buddha position, in the glass case where today's visitors and worshipers can see it.
The temple complex is best reached by taxi or by train (to Sha Tin Station). To the left of the railroad station is a village, through which a path leads up to the temple.

Location
Sha Tin, New Territories

Railway station
Sha Tin

*Tiger Balm Gardens

A kind of Chinese Disneyland, Hong Kong's controversial Tiger Balm Gardens were the creation in 1935 of Aw Boon Haw, who had made a fortune out of selling his "Tiger Balm" ointment. The eight acres of gardens are full of garish plaster figures from Chinese mythology, artificial hills holding caves and grottos, and scenes from life in old China.
The white pagoda, the 165 ft/50 m high symbol of the gardens, is particularly impressive, as well as the palatial mansion of Aw Boon Haw, in traditional Chinese style, which houses his famous collection of jade. The collection can be seen by prior appointment (apply to Hong Kong Tourist Association, tel. 3–671111, or Hong Kong Standard, tel. 5–626111).
In recent years there has been much debate over proposals to demolish the gardens.

Location
Tai Hang Road, Hong Kong

Bus
11

Opening times
Daily 9 a.m.–4 p.m.

◀ *Tiger Balm Gardens*

**Tin Hau Temple R

The Tin Hau Temple, together with the Fook Tak Tse, Shing Wong and Shea Tam temples, forms part of a temple complex in the Yaumati District. The temples were originally built about 1870 on another site but were transferred to their present position in 1876; they were last renovated in 1972.
The Tin Hau Temple is dedicated to the goddess of that name, queen of heaven and patroness of seafarers. She was born about A.D. 960, the daughter of a fisherman, and the legend relates that when her family's junk was sinking during a violent storm she saved it by the exercise of her supernatural powers. She is said also to have healed the sick and to have walked over the surface of the water on a straw mat. Associated with her in the temple are the statues of other divinities.
Hong Kong has several temples dedicated to Tin Hau – e.g. at Aberdeen (Peel Rise) and Stanley (Main Street).

Location
Public Square Street, Kowloon

Buses
1, 2, 6

Opening times
Daily

Tsim Sha Tsui Cultural Centre

The Tsim Sha Tsui Cultural Centre is an ambitious project developed by the municipal administration between 1980 and 1984. The first phase saw the completion in 1980 of the Hong Kong Space Museum (see entry), together with the Planetarium and exhibition and lecture halls.
The center complex also houses a 3000-seat concert hall, a 1500-seat theater, the Hong Kong Museum of History (see entry) and the local government department for arts and recreation.

Location
Salisbury Road, Kowloon

Victoria City (Central District) A–Y

Nowadays called Hong Kong Central District, Victoria, in the central part of the north of the island, is the capital of the Crown Colony and is the bustling heart of its business world. Land here sells at as much as £20,000 a square yard and the skyscrapers with their banks and company offices have almost completely ousted the old buildings of the early colonial days. Looking around at the streets and spacious squares between the Mandarin and Hilton Hotels it is hard to believe that as recently as the 1960s tall white Victorian houses, fronted by verandas, stood here. The fountains and gardens in the broad expanse of Statue Square were only completed in 1966. High-rise blocks have come to dominate this busy quarter, and are also tending to displace the older offices and business premises on the waterfront.
The last remnants of the colonial days are the Supreme Court opposite the War Memorial, the old Officers' Mess, a long, grey two-story building with verandas, east of the Hilton Hotel, St John's Cathedral, built in 1847–49 opposite the Victoria Peak Tramway Station, and Government House, the British Governor's residence on Upper Albert Road. South-west of Government House and separated by Albany Road there are

◀ *Tin Hau, patroness of seafarers, in her temple*

Victoria City: Hong Kong's business center

the Zoological and Botanical Gardens where the Chinese can be seen in the early morning practicing their traditional shadow-boxing. Also included in the older buildings are the de luxe Mandarin Hotel and the Prince's Building alongside, decorated with ceramic reliefs and famous for the quality of its shops.

The most striking building in this district, however, is the Landmark, a 5-story shopping mall with about 100 shops built around a big inner courtyard, complete with fountains, where there is all kinds of free entertainment at weekends.

Queen's Road going westward leads to much more Chinese-looking open shopfronts, etc., while steep and narrow "ladder streets" lead off the main road to the south-west, up the hillside, lined with stalls and tiny shops offering a host of wares. The most picturesque are Ladder Street, with its junk shops, and Cat Street (Upper and Lower Lascar Row) with its curios (see entries). Also worth visiting are the two Taoist temples at 124 Hollywood Road, Man Mo and Lit Shing Kung temples (see entries).

North-east of Queen's Road, Connaught Road runs past the ferry terminals, starting from the Connaught Centre, the tower block which is the home, on the 35th floor, of the Hong Kong Tourist Association (HKTA). The General Post Office is opposite, as well as the Government Publication Centre, which keeps a wide assortment of literature about Hong Kong in its Government Information Service bookshop. City Hall, east of the Connaught Centre, in Edinburgh Place, has three auditoriums for the arts in its Low Block, while the High Block contains the Urban Council offices and, on the 10th and 11th floors, the Hong Kong Museum of Art (see entry). South of City

Hall, on Cotton Tree Drive, is Flagstaff House (see entry), built in 1844, formerly the home of the Commander of the Armed Forces, and now the Museum of Tea, containing Chinese teaware dating from the sixth dynasty to the present. West of City Hall, along Victoria Harbour, are the piers for the various ferries, ranging from the famous Star Ferry for Kowloon, to the new Macau Ferry Pier, where boats and jetfoils leave on the 1–3½ hour journey to the Portuguese territory of Macau. Close by the Poor Man's Night-club (see entry) is a colorful spectacle every evening when this street market gets going and the street-traders set up their stalls, delicious fish specialities are offered for sale, and buskers of all kinds perform for the passers-by. It's worth going for a stroll along the quayside in the daytime, too, and watching the lighters, junks, etc. from the People's Republic of China (mostly out of Canton on the Pearl River) unloading their cargos of foodstuffs, building materials, etc.
South-west of Connaught Road and Queen's Road, on Bonham Road, lies the University of Hong Kong which also houses the Fung Ping Shan Museum (see entry), founded in 1953 and specializing in Chinese ceramics and bronzes.

Victoria Park

C/J

Victoria Park, Hong Kong's municipal park, lies between Victoria Park Road and Causeway Road, to the east of the Causeway Bay shopping center. It has an open-air swimming-pool, tennis-courts, roller-skating rinks and – by the standards of central Hong Kong – unusually large areas of grass and trees. The park is the scene of open-air concerts, cycle races and many cultural events.

Location
Victoria Park Road/
Causeway Road, Hong Kong

Buses
2, 5B, 25

View of Hong Kong harbor from Victoria Peak

The Mid-Autumn Festival in September attracts thousands of people to the park, who come with lanterns to celebrate a form of harvest thanksgiving, with a variety of popular entertainments and an abundance of food and drink.
The park is open daily.

**Victoria Peak S/T

Bus
15

Peak Tramway

Victoria Peak is the highest point on the island of Hong Kong (1818 ft/554 m) and affords the best panoramic views. The upper station of the Peak Tramway is at 1303 ft/397 m, and it is a steep and breath-taking ride of only 8 minutes from the lower station (Murray Building), behind the Hilton Hotel (Garden Road), to the upper one. The Peak Tramway, which has operated since 1888 without a single accident, is one of the Crown Colony's oldest – and safest – means of transport. It is a funicular in which the "up" and "down" cars counterbalance one another, but since there is often a big queue of people waiting to go up, it's worth taking a taxi or minibus to the top and then going back down by the tram.
At the Upper Peak Station are two restaurants and a cafeteria, shops and an observation terrace which affords a magnificent view of the city below, the harbor, Kowloon and the airport, and the hills of the New Territories. In clear weather a walk around the top of the hill, which takes about an hour, is very rewarding. To the south can be seen the offshore islands, and in the evening there are fine sunsets to the west, offering a tempting subject for photographers. The best shots are to be had when darkness falls and the city below becomes a great expanse of twinkling lights.
Formerly only foreigners lived on Victoria Peak. It was not until after the war that Chinese were allowed to settle in this area, which still preserves a number of old colonial buildings.
In spring the peak is often shrouded in mist, and it can be quite chilly, but in the summer it provides a cool respite from the oppressive heat of the city districts down below.

**Wan Chai H/I/P/Q

Location
E of city center, Hong Kong

The Wan Chai district lies to the east of the central area on the island of Hong Kong. It can be reached by way of Queensway or Harcourt Road.
Wan Chai (or Wanchai), the home district of Suzie Wong, the bar girl, in the "Luk Kwok" hotel, of the novel and the movie, is an entertainment quarter, a favorite haunt of seamen, lured there by the bright lights of its bars, discos and night-clubs, and the winking neon advertising its nightlife. During the day it is worth visiting on account of its countless market stalls selling live animals and fresh vegetables. Besides several little temples there is also the 66-story Hopewell Centre and the Arts Centre which stages plays and other shows.
Once a typically Chinese district known as "Little Shanghai", Wan Chai is now steadily losing its original character: the old houses are being pulled down and replaced by tall office blocks, and the ever rising rent levels are compelling many small shopkeepers and businessmen to give up their businesses or to move to much less attractive parts of the city.

West Point

West Point and Western District, situated on Sulphur Channel at the north-west corner of Hong Kong Island, were the first major area settled by the British after their arrival in 1842, and the names of streets and buildings in this densely populated part of the city recall these early arrivals. The farther west you go, however, the more Chinese does the area become: shops and business more rarely advertise their existence in English, and few white-skinned people are to be seen. Here, too, redevelopment and modernization are in progress; but there are still interesting Chinese tea-houses, medicine shops and commercial houses. This is not in any sense a typical tourist area, but a district which will give the stranger an excellent impression of traditional Chinese life.

Location
W end of Hong Kong Island

Buses
5A, 5B

Yau Ma Tei

R

Yau Ma Tei (or Yaumati) is the name of another of Hong Kong's typhoon shelters, and of the adjoining city district. Like Aberdeen and Causeway Bay, it provides a home for large numbers of Chinese boat people (some 8000 people living on 1000 boats), and it is also an anchorage for the lighters which discharge cargo vessels. A trip in a sampan will prove an interesting experience for visitors. Particularly in the evening the boats of the boat dwellers, with their occupants engaged in playing mahjong, celebrating some festival or preparing a meal, present a picturesque spectacle.

In this city district, bounded by Nathan Road in the east, Public Square Street in the north, Temple Street with its Chinese Night Market (see entry) in the west, and Market Street in the south, there are four Chinese temples – Tin Hau (see entry), Fook Tak Tse, Shing Wong and Shea Tam.

The famous jade market (see entry) takes place every day just west of the junction of Kansu Street and Reclamation Street.

Location
W coast of Kowloon, near Jordan Road

Young's Wax Museum

W

This museum presents 3000 years of Chinese history in the form of wax figures of both famous and nameless people from all fields of Chinese life, including Confucius, Genghis Khan, Tzu Hsi, the famous concubine of the Emperor Wen Tsung (Ch'ing dynasty) and Dr Sun Yat-sen, father of the Chinese revolution of 1911 which overthrew the Ch'ing (Manchu) dynasty. The only non-Chinese figure in the museum is Queen Elizabeth II.

Location
Princess Wing of Miramar Hotel, Kimberley Road, Kowloon

Opening times
11 a.m.–7 p.m.

*Zoological and Botanical Garden

M

Founded in 1871 as the Botanical Gardens, these gardens are now managed by the municipal authorities as both a zoo and a botanical garden. They lie quite near the city center

Location
Upper Albert Road/Garden Road, Hong Kong

Zoological and Botanical Garden

Opening times
Daily 6.30 a.m.–10 p.m.

(10 minutes' walk from the Hilton Hotel). The botanical garden contains a representative selection of tropical and subtropical flora, while the small zoo has one of the largest collections of birds in Asia (concentrating on rare and protected species), together with monkeys, jaguars, pumas and various smaller species. A new free-flight aviary with a waterfall was added in 1982. In the early morning visitors can see devotees of the Chinese art of shadow-boxing (tai chi chuan) performing their exercises.

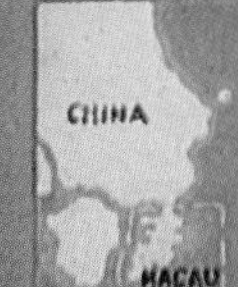
廣東中山縣
CHINA
前山 TSIN SHAN
BARRIER GATE
HOUSE FOR THE POOR
RACE COURSE
TSING CHAU
SPORTS GROUND
CEMETERY
RUINS OF ST. PAUL
RESERVOIR
AIRPORT
NEW HARBOUR
CAU HARBOUR
澳門全圖 MACAU
SCALE. 1:10,000
CHINA
CHINA
NEW TERRITORIES
KOWLOON
MACAU
LANTAO
HONG KONG

Macau

An Men

General

Macau is officially a Chinese territory under Portuguese administration. It gets its Chinese name of Ao Men or An Men from "A Ma Gau", meaning the bay of the Chinese goddess of the sea (also known as Tin Hau). This was shortened to Macau. Located on China's south coast, it is about 40 miles/64 km south-west of Hong Kong, and consists of the Macau peninsula ($2\frac{1}{2}$ miles/4 km long by up to 1 mile/1·7 km wide), with the territory's capital of the same name, and the two islands of Taipa and Coloane which are joined to it by a bridge and a causeway.

Language

Portuguese and Cantonese Chinese are the official languages, but English is also widely spoken.

Capital

The territory's capital is Macau, or to give it its full name "Cidade do São Nome de Deus de Macau, Não Há Outra Mais Leal".

Administration

Since 17 February 1976 the territory of Macau has enjoyed full internal self-government under Portuguese suzerainty. It has a Governor appointed by the Portuguese President, who is assisted by a Consultative Council.
There is a Legislative Council of 17 members, five appointed by the Governor, six directly elected and six indirectly elected. The municipal administration consists of a President, a six-member Council of Elders, two representatives of the Chinese population, two councillors nominated by the government and two representatives of the largest taxpayers.

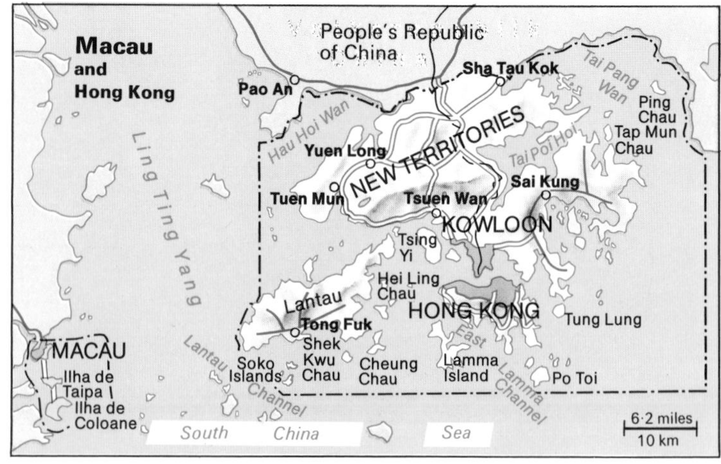

Geographical situation

Like Rome and Lisbon, Macau is built on seven hills. It lies on the west side of the Pearl River Estuary, between latitude 22° 06′ and 22° 13′ N and longitude 113° 33′ and 113° 37′ E.

Climate

Macau has a subtropical climate, with warm to hot temperatures (averaging 82 °F/28 °C for the year), with rainfall at its heaviest from April to October. Cool winds off the sea make the hot season more bearable than in Hong Kong. The winters have less rainfall and colder temperatures (under 68 °F/20 °C) and the weather is at its most agreeable in November and December.

Area and population

Macau has an area of 6 sq. miles/15·5 sq. km, and a population of about 500,000 (66,700 to the sq. mile, or 25,800 to the sq. km). Since the Second World War refugees have been part of the general scene, and generations of them, such as the thousands of boat people living on the sea of junks in the Porto Interior, the inner harbor, have known no other way of life. Although both China and Macau have taken steps to halt the flow of refugees from the People's Republic, and although Macau offers little in the way of economic prospects to newcomers, in recent years the population has continued to increase.

International direct dialing

The international direct dialing code for Macau is 853 followed by the subscriber's number.

Population and Religion

Population

Macau's population is 98 per cent Chinese, the rest being Portuguese or of mixed blood (Macaenses). Almost a third of the population consists of refugees who fled from the Japanese forces occupying China and Hong Kong during the Second World War, or left China during Mao Tse Tung's Cultural Revolution. Ten per cent of Macau's inhabitants are boat people, living on the water.

Religion

Although Macau is the see of a Roman Catholic bishop, only about 25,000 of its people are Roman Catholic, with the overwhelming majority of the population being Buddhist (76 per cent). The alternation of magnificent Church processions with Chinese festivals is a testimony to the religious freedom that is possible with a peaceful coexistence of Eastern and Western religions.

Transport

Macau has yet to gain its independence so far as transport and communications are concerned. Silting-up of the harbor on the Pearl River and keen competition from Hong Kong led to its losing its significance as a trading post between China and the West, although the harbor is currently being extended and a container terminal is being built, thanks to the investment that has flowed into Macau with its opening up to mainland China. Nevertheless all overseas traffic is via Hong Kong, and regular ferry services ply between the two territories, using jetfoils,

hovercraft, etc. These carried 9,255,890 passengers in 1985. Taxis and buses run from the landing-stage in the Porto Exterior, the outer harbor, to the city center where most of the hotels are located. The Porto Interior, Macau's inner harbor and typhoon shelter, is on the west side of the peninsula.
Since 1979 there has been a helicopter link with Hong Kong, and a start is due to be made in 1990 on building a STOL port that would link in with the rest of the international air traffic network.
An important road-link within Macau is the 1·6 mile/2·6 km bridge from the mainland to the island of Taipa where a new industrial zone has sprung up.

Culture

Like Hong Kong, Macau is a city of contrasts, where East meets West to give a mixture of native Chinese shops and dwellings, monumental European and Asian holy buildings for the different religions and elegant villas in a style reminiscent of southern Europe.
The oldest parts of town in the low-lying areas safe from typhoons look like a Portuguese country town, with squat rows of houses lining cobbled streets. The rain-bleached façades of these one-time prosperous 18th c. houses, with their Rococo dormer-windows, graceful pillars and ornate balconies, hint at their past elegance. In the packed shopping streets, with ideographs strung from house to house, there are craftsmen's and tailors' modest little workshops, where scholars who can also cast horoscopes set up their tiny tables beside modern shopping arcades that bear witness to the advancing tide of the 20th c.
Macau has also recently gained a university, the University of East Asia on Taipa. Currently theater companies that are visiting Hong Kong also give performances in Macau, mainly in the Teatro de Dom Pedro. Fado and folk-dance from Portugal are also both regular forms of entertainment, while exhibitions are put on from time to time in the Luis de Camões Museum, the Historical Archives, National Library and Military Museum.
About 30 Chinese, Christian and historic festivals and sporting events throughout the year make for a lively and varied events calendar.

Commerce and Industry

The territory's economy is largely based on textile and clothing manufacture, although textiles in particular have been hard hit by American import restrictions. Other developing industries are plastics, electronics, leather goods, optical goods and fireworks. These mostly take the form of small and medium-sized companies. Tourism plays a big part in Macau's economy (4 million visitors in 1984), particularly by Hong Kong Chinese who come to gamble in the casinos which are banned in the Crown Colony and account for 20 per cent of the gross national product.
Another major source of revenue is gold trading, which is a State monopoly.

There has been a shift in mainland China's economic policy to the south of the country, as is apparent from the infrastructural investment and industrial location in the Chinese "Special Economic Zone" of Zhuhai which borders Macau in the north. This economic advance has also had an impact on Macau where telecommunications and transportation systems have been improved and where, for example, the harbor is being extended and a new cement plant is being built that will also serve China and Hong Kong.
Macau has to import most of its foodstuffs, apart from fish, from the People's Republic, since its own farming produces only 8 per cent of what it needs, so there is clearly a need for economic diversification. In 1983 the gross national product amounted to 780 million dollars, i.e. 2560 dollars per head of population.

History

Jorge Álvares becomes the first European to reach the Pearl River delta. 1513

After some skirmishing the mandarins ruling the province of Canton lease the territory of Macau to the Portuguese. 1557

Founding of the diocese. 1575

Trade with China and Japan makes Macau the richest city in the Far East. 1595–1602

Attacks by an Anglo-Dutch fleet are successfully repulsed. Macau becomes a popular summer retreat for Canton's wealthy merchants, the taipans. 1604–27

The Opium War damages Macau's trade. Many Portuguese leave the city. 1842

Macau is hived off from the Portuguese colonial territory of Goa and forms a new province together with Timor and Solor. 1844

Macau becomes a free port, the status which it still enjoys today, and is no longer obliged to pay duties to the Chinese on imports, turnover, etc. 1845

The new Governor, Joao Ferreira do Amaral drives out the Chinese tax-collectors. 1846

Under the Sino–Portuguese Treaty of Tientsin Macau is recognized as a purely Portuguese province. 1862

China ratifies the 1862 treaty, and concludes a friendship and trade treaty with Portugal. Portugal receives sovereignty over Macao, Taipa and Coloane provided the islands are never disposed of without China's consent. 1887

Macao becomes a favorite summer resort with British merchants. *c.* 1900

Macau's neutrality means it is spared by the Japanese. The great influx of refugees swells the population to half a million. 1941–45

Macau – History

1951	Macau is declared a Portuguese overseas province.
1966	Demonstrations in favor of the People's Republic of China leave many dead and injured.
1974	Following the bloodless overthrow of Salazar, the Portuguese dictator, Lisbon's new Socialist government makes a vain attempt to give Macau back to China but China is reluctant to do away with this outlet for international trade; the political uncertainty acts as a damper on willingness to invest.
1975	Portugal disbands its colonial empire.
February 1976	Macau gets a new statute guaranteeing its internal independence as a Chinese territory under Portuguese administration.
1982	Four-year textile agreement with the European Community.
1985	Agreement is reached between the People's Republic of China and Portugal to commence official negotiations on the future of Macau at an early opportunity.
1986	Portugal's new President, Mario Soares, also wants to see Macau "return to the Middle Kingdom", and new negotiations are scheduled for late summer. Talks are held between Zhou Nan from the Chinese Foreign Office, and the Portuguese envoy Ruy Barbosa Medina. The issue remains whether Macau should be culturally, economically and politically brought into line – "solucao sincronizado" – with Hong Kong by the Chinese in 1997, coming under China as an autonomous special zone as well.

Macau from A to Z

*A-Ma Miu (temple)

Location
Barra Point

The Temple of A-Ma Miu, or Ma Kok Miu Temple, as it is also known, is dedicated to A-Ma (Tin Hau by another name), the goddess of the sea and patron saint of seafarers and fishermen. It is the most picturesque temple in Macau, and actually gave its name to the settlement, which was called "A-Ma-Gau" (A-Ma's Bay) by the first Portuguese settlers in 1557. It stands at the foot of the Barra and Penha hills in south-west Macau. A Chinese inscription records that it was built under the Ming

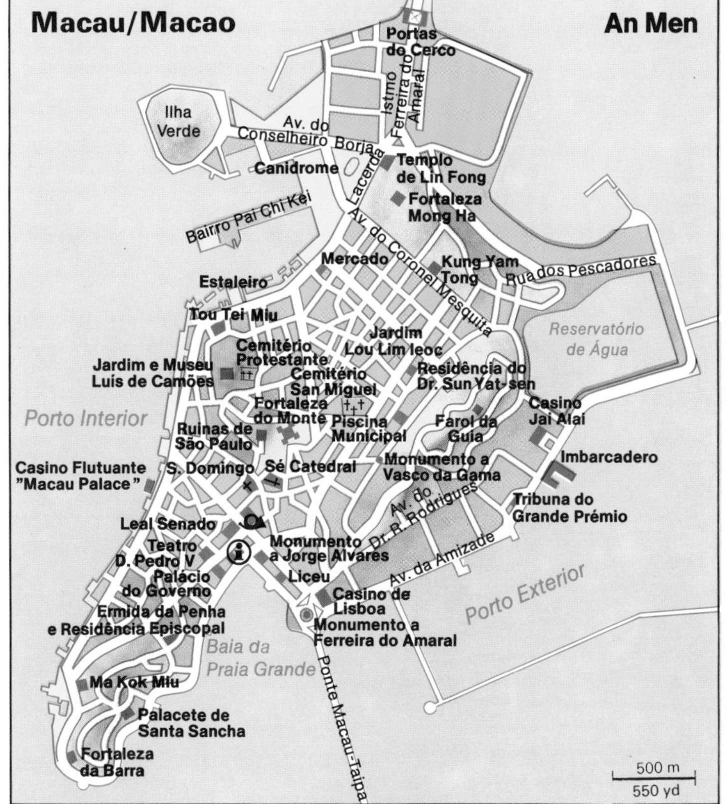

dynasty by the Emperor Wa Li (1573–1621). It seems at some stage to have been partly destroyed, for another inscription states that it was rebuilt in the reign of Tuo Keung (1824–56). The giant boulders on the hillside around the temple are inscribed with red calligraphy telling the story of the goddess who was supposed to have saved a humble junk from a storm.

Avenida Almeida Ribeiro

This 1920s street of shops passes through an old Chinese quarter full of wonderfully colorful shopping arcades.

** Baia da Praia Grande

This bay, a favorite subject for artists in the 19th c., extends from the Lisboa Hotel to the promontory at the other end. Lined with picturesque old buildings, each with a history of its own, it takes the spectator right back to the last century.

In the Avenida da Amizade, the street running parallel to the coast, in front of the Lisboa Hotel, stands a monument to Governor Ferreira do Amaral. At the junction of the Avenida da Amizade with Rua de Praia Grande is a monument to Jorge Álvares, the first European to set foot on Chinese soil. Farther down the street, on the right, we come to Government Palace (Palácio do Governo), and in a street off the Avenida da República on the right is the Governor's Residence (Palacete de Santa Sancha).

In the Baia da Praia Grande: Government Palace . . .

... and the Governor's Residence

Canidrome (greyhound stadium)

Greyhound-racing takes place at this splendidly named dogtrack on Tuesdays, Saturdays and Sundays.

Location
Av. General Castelo Branco

**Casino de Lisboa

Macau owes its reputation as the Oriental answer to Las Vegas and Monte Carlo largely to this casino housed on two floors in the Hotel Lisboa, with 600 beds Macau's biggest hotel. Here gamblers can indulge their passion 24 hours a day, and many of Macau's visitors are here just for the casinos. A whole month's wages can be staked – and, as often as not, lost – on "Fan Tu" or "Dai Siu". To make sure that guests settle their bills almost all the hotels insist on being paid in advance. The second largest casino, the Palacio de Macau, is usually known as "Casino Flutuante", the floating casino, since it is to be found on a converted ferry off the Rua das Lorchas in the inner harbor.

The Jai Alai Casino sees the world's fastest betting and, in "Jai Alai", the world's fastest ballgame, while the Kam Pek Casino in the center of town caters only for Chinese gaming and is patronized largely by the locals.

Not far from the Casino de Lisboa entrance there is a monument to Governor Ferreira do Amaral, the founder of independent Macau.

Location
Hotel Lisboa, Avenida da Amizade

Opening times
Daily, 24 hours a day

葡京大酒店
ESTORIL TOURS
191

Churches

Macau has many Roman Catholic churches, but they are only open during church services on Sundays. However, the outside of the churches, which span four centuries, are well worth looking at. The following are among the most interesting:
St Anthony's Church, Rua de Santo António, founded 1558, altered and renovated in 1608, 1809, 1875 and 1940;
St Augustine's Church, Largo de Santo Agostinho, founded 1586, rebuilt 1814, altered 1875;
St Dominic's Church, Largo de São Domingos, founded about 1580 and rebuilt in the Baroque style by the Dominicans in the 17th c.;
St Lazarus' Church, Calcada da Ig. de S. Lázaro, built 1885, renovated 1966, shows traces of Baroque;
St Lawrence's Church, Rua de São Lourenco, first built in the 16th c., rebuilt and altered several times in the 19th c., with immediately behind it St Joseph's Seminar, dating from between 1746 and 1758, where the Museum of Religious Art is being assembled.
See Sé Cathedral.

Coloane

Coloane is the second of Macau's offshore islands, reached from the mainland by way of the Taipa Bridge and a two-lane causeway from Taipa built in 1969 and extending for $1\frac{1}{2}$ miles/ 2·3 km. Almost twice the size of Taipa (see entry), it is an island of large pine forests, eucalyptus groves, tropical vegetation and farmland. The Tam Kong Temple near the entrance to the Pousada Miramar is worth a visit to see its famous whalebone model of a ship with a wooden dragon's head at its prow. From here, across a narrow channel, there is a good view of the People's Republic of China.
Coloane is famous for its beautiful beaches of fine white sand. There are three particularly worth recommending – Cheoc Van in the south with two "pousadas", or inns, and a park open from 9 a.m. to 10 p.m. with a restaurant and swimming-pool, and, under construction, a leisure center for the crews from the oilrigs in the South China Sea; Hac Sa, in the east of the island, has Coloane Park, opened in 1985 with Chinese pavilions and tropical gardens, near the beach, open from 9 a.m. to 7 p.m. daily, as well as the Hac Sa Sports and Recreation Complex, with tennis-courts, swimming-pool, minigolf, etc. This is open from 9 a.m. to 10 p.m. and charges for admission. The third of these beaches is Baia de Lazaro in the north of the island.
The village of Coloane is a mixture of old Chinese and Portuguese buildings. It has a charming little chapel dedicated to St Francis Xavier, in front of which is a monument commemorating a successful Portuguese action against pirates in 1920.

◄ *Lisboa Hotel, a Mecca for gamblers*

*Ermida da Penha (Church of the Penha) and Residência Episcopal (Bishop's Palace)

Location
Colina de Penha

The Penha Church stands on top of the Penha Hill in southwest Macau, from which there are good views of the Pearl River delta and the Chinese mainland. A chapel was originally built here in 1622 by the passengers and crew of the "São Bartolomeu", which had had a narrow escape from capture by Dutch freebooters. For many years it was occupied as a hermitage. The present church dates from 1935.

Adjoining the church is the Bishop's Palace.

Fortaleza da Barra (fortress)

Location
Avenida da República

This fortress was built in 1629 and originally its commandant was directly appointed by the King of Portugal. It was enlarged in 1740 and since 1982 its outer walls, which are all that remain, have contained the Pousada da Barra, a small luxury hotel.

Fortaleza do Mong Ha (fortress)

Location
Mong Ha Hill

This fortress, which was considered impregnable, was built by Governor Ferreira do Amaral in 1844. There has been a hotel here, and Macau's school of tourism, since 1982. There is also a good view of the distant Chinese mainland.

*Fortaleza do Monte (Old Monte Fort)

Location
Rua do Monte

The Fortaleza do Monte was completed in 1626 by the Jesuits. Later it was taken over by Governor Dom Francisco Mascarenhas, who made it his official residence. It remained the governor's residence until 1746.

In 1622, while the fort was still under construction, the Dutch attacked Macau at this point, but suffered an annihilating defeat at the hands of the valiant churchmen, under the leadership of Adam Schell von Bell and Jerónimo Rio.

There is now a weather station in the fort.

Government Palace (Palacio do Governo)

Location
Bahia da Praia Grande

Macau's seat of govenment, the Palacio do Governo, is a very impressive pink and white classical mansion (see Baia da Praia Grande). Its three wings were built in 1849 by Macau's foremost architect, Tomas de Aquino, and they contain the offices of the Governor and his Ministers.

Guia Fort and Lighthouse

The Farol da Guia, built in 1627, is the highest point in Macau and has wonderful views out over the whole of the territory and the broad estuary of the Pearl River. Inside the fort there is the typically Portuguese Chapel of Our Lady of Guia, built in 1707, and the lighthouse which dates from 1865 and is the oldest on the China coast.

Location
Estrado do Engebheiro Trigo, Guia Hill

Jai Alai Stadium

This spectacular stadium opposite the ferry wharf, can take 5000 spectators. Jai Alai is similar to the Basque game of pelota and is said to be the fastest ballgame in the world. The games begin at 7.30 p.m. every night and last until midnight, and there are additional sessions at 2 p.m. on public holidays and at weekends.

Location
Avenida do Rodrigo Rodrigues

**Kun Iam Tong (Temple)

This labyrinthine Buddhist temple dedicated to the goddess of mercy, also known as the Kwan Yiu, was built in 1627; its name appears for the first time, however, under the Yuan dynasty (1279–1368). In the entrance hall are three figures of the Buddha, representing the past, the present and the future. In another hall is the Goddess of Mercy, flanked on either side by nine Buddhas.

It was on the stone table in the beautiful garden in the courtyard that the first Sino-American Treaty was signed on 3 July 1844 by the Viceroy of Canton and United States Envoy Caleb Cushing. There are some fine porcelain reliefs and roof-figures from the Ming period. One of the many gold-lacquered Buddhas is supposed to have the features of Marco Polo, one of China's 18 wise men.

The "Tree of the Loving Couples" is where young lovers pray for future happiness.

Location
Avenida do Coronel Mesquita

Kwan Tai Miu (Temple)

This temple in the heart of the busy market of São Domingos was built in 1860 and is dedicated to Kwan Tai, the god of war, whose statue is on the altar.

Location
Mercado de São Domingos

*Leal Senado (Loyal Senate)

The Avenida Almeida Ribeiro, Macau's main street, gives on to the Largo do Leal Senado, the European-style square on which stands the imposing Senate building. It is known as the "loyal" Senate because the Senate of 1809 sent a man-of-war to help out the Portuguese court when it fled from Napoleon's troops to Brazil. The present building is a superb example of colonial

Location
Avenida de Almeida Ribeiro

architecture that supposedly replaced an earlier building in 1784. The elegant façade dates from 1876 and the whole building was restored in 1939–40. From 1585 to 1835 the Senate played a crucial role in Macau's relations with the Chinese government.

On the first floor of the building is the Senate Library, or National Library, with more than 50,000 volumes and manuscripts, including many valuable books up to 500 years old.

In the vicinity of the Senate are many small shops, antique dealers and the Post Office.

*Lin Fong Miu (Temple)

Location
Avenida do Almirante Lacerda

The Lin Fong Miu, or Lotus Temple, was built by Taoists in 1592, and long served as a staging point for travelers to China. It was both the residence and the office of the South Chinese mandarins, who rested here in the course of their long journeys. In front of the temple is a garden, the entrance to which is guarded by stone figures of fabulous animals from Chinese mythology.

Lin Kai Miu (Temple)

Location
Travessa da Corda

The main hall of Lin Kai (stream of sorrow) was built in the 17th c. in honor of Ua Kuong, a Taoist divinity that protects against fires; other parts of the temple are dedicated to Kun Iam, goddess of mercy, and Kwan Tai, god of war.

Lou Lim Ioc Garden

Location
Avenida Conselheiro Ferreira de Almeida

This classic Chinese garden was laid out at the end of the 19th c. by a wealthy Chinese merchant. It is modeled on those of old Soochow, and is a miniaturized landscape with artificial hills and water features. Farther along the Avenida is "Restoration Row", a prize-winning conversion to modern uses of a mixture of older Mediterranean- and Asian-style buildings.

Macau Forum

Location
Outer Harbour Ferry Terminal

Opened in 1985, the Forum is a sports and leisure complex in two air-conditioned buildings complete with sporting and conference facilities, theater, movie theater, bars, cafés, restaurants, exhibition rooms, shops, etc.

*Ma Kok Miu (Temple)

See A-Ma Miu

Monumento a Vasca da Gama

This monument to the great Portuguese navigator and discoverer Vasco da Gama was set up in 1911. At his feet is the sea monster Adamaster, which prophesied ill success for the first Portuguese voyage around the Cape of Good Hope. Undeterred, however, the Portuguese seamen set out in 1497 and discovered the sea route to India.

Location
Rua Ferreiro do Amaral

** Museu Luís de Camões (Camoens Museum)

The Camoens Museum has one of the most valuable art collections in East Asia, with exhibits dating back more than 200 years. The original building, erected about 1770, was for a long time the headquarters of the East India Company. The museum was established in 1940, at first occupying only two rooms; then in 1960 the whole building was converted into a museum. Among the most notable exhibits are a bronze temple drum of the Han dynasty, enamels of the Ch'ing dynasty, monochrome and polychrome pottery and porcelain from the Ming period to the 19th c., arms and armor, palanquins and pictures. (There is a charge for admission, except on Fridays.) The garden behind the museum, on a low hill, also bears the name of the great Portuguese poet Luís Vaz de Camões (1524–80). From the hill there is a particularly fine view of Macau.

Location
Praça Luís de Camões

Opening times
Mon., Tues. and Thurs.–Sun.
10 a.m.–5 p.m.

Closed
Wed. and public holidays

Museu Luís de Camões

Frontier crossing into China

Camões was born in Lisbon, lost his right eye in the Battle of Ceuta (1547) and was thrown into prison in 1553 after fighting a duel. Given the choice between remaining in prison in Portugal or going to one of the Portuguese overseas possessions, he chose the latter and was sent to Goa, where he again got into trouble. Thereafter he is believed to have gone to Macau, where he was given a post as "purveyor of the dead and absent in China". During his stay in Macau he is said to have written his great epic poem "Os Lusiadas" in a cave which now bears his name. There is no documentary evidence, however, that Camões ever actually lived in Macau.

The bronze bust of Camões, with lines from his epic inscribed on the base, is by M. M. Bordalo Pinheiro (1886); it replaces an earlier head of the poet.

In front of the museum is a statue of Count Bernardino de Senna Fernandes, erected in the 19th c. by the Chinese merchants whom he had protected and assisted.

The Old Protestant Cemetery beside the museum was established in 1814 and was the first piece of land in Macau to be owned by foreigners, largely due to the efforts of Dr Robert Morrison, the missionary who for many years acted on behalf of the East India Company, and who translated the Bible into Chinese and published the first English/Chinese dictionary. The 162 gravestones bear fascinating witness to the past, especially in respect of the dead left behind by Commodore Perry's historic fleet.

Old Protestant Cemetery

See Museu Luís de Camões

Palacio do Governo

See Government Palace

** Portas do Cerco (Border Gate)

Location
On Chinese frontier

This gate, the point of entry into the People's Republic of China, was built by the Portuguese in 1870, replacing an earlier gate erected on the frontier by the Chinese. On the Macau side of the gate are inscriptions of military significance and quotations from Camões. Visitors can approach to within 100 yards of the gate. In the square on the Macau side of the frontier are souvenir shops catering for the tourist market.

** Residência do Dr Sun Yat-sen (Dr Sun Yat-sen Memorial House)

Location
Avenida Sidónio Pais

This Moorish-style house was built to commemorate the founder of the Chinese Republic after the house in which he

Sun Yat-sen Memorial House

Ruins of St Paul's Church, seen from the Fortaleza do Monte

Opening times
Mon.–Fri. 10 a.m.–1 p.m.,
Sat. and Sun. 10 a.m.–1 p.m.
and 3–5 p.m.

Closed
Tues.

had lived and practiced as a doctor (and which had thereafter been used as an explosives store) was accidentally blown up in the 1930s.

The new house contains documents on Sun Yat-sen's life and interesting photographs of Chiang Kai-shek, founder of the Republic of China (Taiwan).

Sun Yat-sen, leader of the Kuomintang, a democratic nationalist party which declared war on the corrupt great landowners of the time, proclaimed the Chinese Republic in 1912 after the overthrow of the Manchu dynasty. He is honored as a liberator both by the People's Republic of China and by the Taiwan government.

** Ruinas de São Paulo (Ruins of St Paul's Church)

Location
Rua de São Paulo

All that is left of St Paul's Church, a popular symbol of Macau and at one time "the greatest church in Asia", is the imposing Renaissance façade at the top of a broad flight of granite steps. It was built between 1602 and 1627 by Japanese Christians and local craftsmen on the lines of Il Gesù in Rome after the destruction by fire of an earlier church. The design was by Father Carlo Spinola, later martyred in Japan, and the carved Baroque figures range from the Virgin to skeletons, dragons and other Asian ornamentation. The Jesuits added a college but after their expulsion from Macau in 1762 the church fell into disuse. Troops were billeted in the college in 1831 then in 1835 the church and the college were destroyed by a typhoon and a fire, leaving only the flight of steps and the façade. The most valuable library in Africa and the Orient was also lost in the flames. Attempts were made in 1904 to try and get the church rebuilt, but so far nothing has come of them.

Santa Casa da Misericórdia (Holy House of Mercy)

Location
Largo do Senado

The "Holy House of Mercy" at the north end of the Largo do Senado was founded in 1569 by the first Bishop of China and Japan, the Jesuit Dom Melchior Nunes Cameiro Leitão, and the Bishop's cross and skull are on show in a reception room on the second floor. The building is the headquarters of the first Western charity in Asia (1498), and it still provides care for orphans, the sick and the aged, as well as free meals daily for the poor.
Paintings that can be seen in the Santa Casa include portraits of Dom Melchior, Francisco Xavier Roquette and Vincente Jozé Pereira (two of the institution's principal supporters), and its Chinese benefactress Marta Merop.

* Sé Catedral (Cathedral)

Location
Largo da Sé

Opening times
Daily at 5.30 p.m. (for service)

The Cathedral, designed by J. T. da Aquino, was built in 1844–50 and reconstructed in 1938. It occupies the site of an earlier church which was destroyed by a typhoon in 1836.
The building is of basilican type, with two sturdy towers and large and heavy doorways. In a shrine above the chapel are the relics of Japanese martyrs who died during the persecution of Christians in Japan in the early 17th c.

Taipa

The island of Taipa, now linked with Macau by a bridge, is being developed as a new industrial center. Formerly a Chinese customs post for all vessels putting in at Macau, it also had fireworks factories and a certain amount of fishing.
Chinese shops and Portuguese colonial buildings are the main features of Taipa's townscape. In the north-west section of the island is the new hilltop University of East Asia, with its three faculties of arts and sciences.
The year 1980 saw the opening of the Raceway of the Macau Trotting Club, which has a capacity of 15,000 and attracts hordes of gambling and racing enthusiasts every Sunday. At the end of the track there is a "four-faced" Buddhist shrine, only the third of its kind in the world, the other two being in Bangkok and Las Vegas.
On the island there are five small Chinese temples, the best known of which is the Tin Hau Temple, now a secondary school. Built some 180 years ago, it has a highly ornamented shrine containing a figure of the goddess. Near by is the Pak Tai Temple, built 120 years ago in the time of the Emperor Tao

Kuang, which is notable for its rich decoration and for two life-size guardian figures formed from a clay-like substance.
Farther away, beyond the fireworks factories, is the Kwan Tai Temple, with its lovely little miniature temple that is carried in processions.
The Kun Iam Temple, on the north coast of the island, is very unusual in design since it is built against a cliff with the entrance facing out to sea.
The Taipa Folklore Museum was opened in 1985. It is the first of five buildings that are intended to form a "culture" village; the two galleries, craft museum and restaurant specializing in Macau dishes are still under construction.
There is a fine panoramic view from the Church of Senhora do Carmo. The "Taipa Mirador", 1986, is the work of the sculptor Castelo-Branco, who decorated the structure's six walls with symbolic representations of scenes from the daily life of the people over the last four centuries.

Tai Soi Miu (Temple)

Location
Rua de Figeira

This 200-year-old temple "of the sleeping Buddha" is not far from St Paul's Church, and contains a shrine to Pan Kung, the Taoist god of justice, and some fine woodcarvings with bird motifs.

*Teatro de Dom Pedro

Location
Largo de Santo Agostinho

This colonnaded neo-classical theater near Government House is used for the performances of drama and opera which are occasionally given in Macau. The auditorium is oval in plan, with a balcony, and its velvet and plush appointments give it an intimate atmosphere. It is part of the Macau Club, the oldest club in the Far East (men only). The interior has been restored and still reflects the splendors of an earlier period.

Practical Information

Airlines

Airlines of most importance to Western visitors

Air France (AF)
Mandarin Hotel Arcade, Hong Kong, tel. 5–248145
Peninsula Hotel Arcade, Kowloon, tel. 3–684902

Alitalia (AZ)
Hilton Hotel, Hong Kong, tel. 5–237047

British Airways (BA)
Alexandra House, Chater Road, Hong Kong, tel. 5–775023
Royal Garden Hotel (1st floor), Kowloon

British Caledonian Airways
14th Floor, South China Building,
1–3 Wyndham Street, Hong Kong Central, tel. 5–212353

Cathay Pacific (CX)
Swire House, Hong Kong, tel. 5–640123
Peninsula Hotel Arcade, Kowloon, tel. 3–662407

Lufthansa (LH)
Hilton Hotel, Hong Kong, tel 5–212311
Peninsula Hotel Arcade, Kowloon, tel. 3–662025

Pan American (PA)
Alexandra House, Chater Road, Hong Kong, tel. 5–231111
Peninsula Hotel Arcade, Kowloon, tel. 3–687171

Singapore Airlines (SQ)
Keyamally Building, Hong Kong, tel. 5–202233
Peninsula Hotel Arcade, Kowloon, tel. 3–674104

Swissair (SR)
New Henry House, Hong Kong, tel. 5–293670
Peninsula Hotel Arcade, Kowloon, tel. 3–687040

Thai International (TG)
New Henry House, Hong Kong, tel. 5–295601
Peninsula Hotel Arcade, Kowloon, tel. 3–664593

Other airlines include relative newcomers such as Hong Kong Dragon Airlines and Oriental Pearls Airways.

It is very important to confirm your return flight 72 hours before it is due to depart.

Airport

Hong Kong has an international airport at Kai Tak, which is used by more than 40 international airlines and has daily connections with countries all over the world. The airport lies on the outskirts of central Kowloon and can easily be reached

Buses
From Hong Kong Island
No. 200, 7.30 a.m.–10.45 p.m.

From Kowloon
No. 201, 8 a.m.–10.30 p.m.

from Hong Kong Island in half an hour and from the Kowloon hotels in 15 minutes. Passengers are requested to check in at the airport $1\frac{1}{2}$ hours before departure.
There are duty-free shopping facilities for outgoing passengers. An airport tax (now HK $100) is payable on departure.
All passengers and baggage must pass through stringent security controls.
There are no luggage lockers, but there is a left luggage office in the departure hall, opposite the Pan American desk (open daily 7.15 a.m.–11.30 p.m.).
Since there are no conveyor belts even heavy hand baggage has to be carried for considerable distances.

Air travel

More than 95 per cent of all visitors to Hong Kong come by air, and the colony is a paradise for those in quest of cheap fares. If you want to visit a neighboring country you should apply to one of Hong Kong's many travel agencies, which have agreements with individual airlines for the sale of tickets at reduced prices. You should never buy your ticket from the airline itself, for if you do you will pay considerably more. Cathay Pacific, Singapore Airlines, Malaysian Airlines System, Thai International and China Airlines all issue reduced-price tickets through travel agencies.
Popular destinations from Hong Kong, with reasonably priced fares, are Tokyo (Japan), Kuala Lumpur (Malaysia), Manila (Philippines), Indonesia, Bali and Thailand.
Since 1979 there has also been a helicopter service to Macau.
See Airlines and Travel agencies.

Antiques

Genuine and valuable antiques are to be found almost exclusively in the more up-market shops. Particularly in the case of Chinese objects, age is not necessarily the determining factor in assessing value: frequently the products of a later dynasty are more valuable than similar items belonging to an earlier one. The expert is able to shift the gold out of the immense amount of dross, but the less experienced buyer should beware of alleged antiques which are not infrequently worthless imitations and rely instead on some of the very attractive craft products which are also available, often based on older models.

Ivory

Old ivory is rare and extremely expensive. The older the ivory the more it tends to take on a brownish tinge in place of its original cream colour. Hong Kong is an international center of ivory-working; but since the raw material is in increasingly short supply prices continue to rise. Accordingly ivory has in recent years become a form of capital investment.
Countless reproductions of old Chinese motifs are offered for sale in Hong Kong, and some of the counterfeits are difficult even for experts to detect. The only safe plan, therefore, is to buy from reputable shops. One simple test can be applied, though even this is not 100 per cent foolproof: genuine ivory is not harmed by the flame of a cigarette-lighter, while an imitation will be blackened and distorted.

Gemstones and jewelry

Allow yourself plenty of time if you want to buy gemstones or jewelry, and look for a jeweler who is a member of an official tourist association or a similar body. Before examining an item that is being offered for sale ask the jeweler to lend you his magnifying glass. This kind of lens has a very short focal length, and objects should be viewed from a distance of between 1 and 2 inches/1·5 and 2·5 cm. Check whether the setting of the stone you have chosen is too loose or even so tight that the stone will get damaged. Check whether the setting is covering up defects in the stone, whether the stone has been properly cut and polished.

With precious metals, check their marks. Gold or gold-alloyed items should have marks indicating both the gold fineness (expressed in carats) of the article, and the identity of the shop or manufacturer. Pure gold is 24 carats, while 22 carat means 22 part gold to 2 parts of a lesser metal, usually copper or silver. Fineness is often also expressed in mils, so that, for example, 14 carat is equivalent to 585 mils. For silver the fineness should be at least 90 per cent; the proportion of pure silver in sterling silver is 925 mils.

When negotiating a price with a jeweler it is important to deal with the price of the stone and the setting separately. Even the experts can have difficulty with pricing since the current market price will be determined by factors such as fashion, temporary shortages, etc.

When buying gemstones check on the famous "Four Cs" – color, clarity, cut and carat-weight (unlike precious metals, carat in stones is a measure of weight).

With color, check whether the stone is too dark or too pale (diamonds, for instance, are particularly valuable if they are not clouded in any way; a yellowish tinge is a sure sign of poorer quality, except when the stones have pure, strong colours like yellow, brandy-brown, rose, green or blue). You should also remember that the color of a stone can appear to vary according to the lighting in the jeweler's shop.

Clarity: check whether the stone is free of any flaws. The experts call a stone flawless, or lens-perfect, if nothing can be detected even through a magnifying glass with a ×10 magnification. Emeralds, rubies and sapphires can have tiny flaws.

Cut: check whether the stone is bright and shining, or whether it seems dull and lustreless, in which case this may be because it has been wrongly cut so that the light is being refracted towards the back of the stone instead of out towards the person looking at it.

Carat-weight: 1 metric carat equals 200 milligrams. Further subdivision is into cents, which are normally expressed as "points", so that a ½ carat stone could be said to weigh "50" points.

You should also check whether a stone is natural or synthetic. For some time now it has been possible to make certain gemstones such as emeralds, rubies, sapphires and spinel in the laboratory, and these synthetic stones will have the same chemical composition and crystal structure as their natural equivalents. There are also synthetic materials used for jewelry which have no natural counterpart, such as titanium, etc.

There are also poorer imitations on the market that are like precious stones in outward appearance only, such as coloured glass, ceramic compounds and synthetic resins. Composite stones fall into a similar category. These are made up of two

(doublets) or, less frequently, three (triplets) sections which have been stuck together, a technique which can produce a very convincing imitation of, say, emerald, which is a green kind of beryl, by gluing two transparent slivers together of the cheaper beryl with a green adhesive, in which case the setting is usually designed to hide the join.
There is basically nothing against synthetic or imitation gemstones so long as they are clearly identified as such.
You should be particularly on your guard with "special offers", although it has to be said that customers only get what they pay for. An aquamarine on offer for $15 is obviously suspect when aquamarines of the right color are worth at least $100 a carat.
If having followed all this advice you still want to be doubly sure you should take the item you're interested in to a laboratory for testing precious stones. When making a purchase insist on a certificate of authenticity, on the firm's headed paper, and containing the following information:
- the full price and a description of the form or style;
- the precious metal content of the setting;
- a precise description of the stones with their approximate weight;
- the signature of the jeweler.

Without a certificate of this kind you cannot claim a refund or get an exchange.

Jade

The ancient Chinese called this mineral "yu", and were already working it as early as about 1000 B.C. The oldest form of the Chinese ideograph for "king" was shaped like a chain of jade. People from many cultures have treasured jade as one of the most popular of their gemstones, but it has probably never been in such great demand as it is nowadays. There are really only two types of mineral that can be called "jade". These are nephrite and jadeite.
Nephrite, known as "the stone of heaven", or Taiwan or New Zealand jade, is mainly found in Tsinyang, Siberia, New Zealand and Canada. Relatively little is found in Taiwan, but much of the Canadian jade is sent there to be worked. Nephritic jade is normally dark green, but paler shades of green are also found. Yellow jade is a yellowish or gray-brown nephrite which has got its coloring from the yellow Chinese clay it is found in.
Jadeite is rarer and more valuable than nephrite, and is also known as Burmese jade since the only place where it is found in any worthwhile quantities is Burma. It varies in color from very pale green to dark green, brown, red, orange, yellow, lilac and black, and is often speckled, frequently with bright green veining or flecks on a white background. The valuable emerald-green jade, which can be either nephrite or jadeite, is known as Chinese jade.
Because of jade's great popularity it is imitated in a great many forms. These include:
- New jade (bowenite, a hard kind of serpentine)
- Indian jade (a green aventurine quartz, recognized by its shining flecks)
- Australian jade (an apple-green chrysopras-quartz)
- Jaspis-jade (green jasper, an impure kind of quartz)
- Amazon jade (blue-green microline felspar)
- Fuyan, Manchurian or Henan jade (saponite, better known as soapstone and identifiable by its softness, with a surface that can be scratched by running a finger-nail over it).

All these stones are among the less valuable look-alikes that Asia's street-traders try to palm off on tourists, since imitation jade is probably the "precious stone" most offered for sale on the street. See A–Z, Jade Market.

Porcelain

Of particular value and rarity is the "blue-and-white" ware produced in the heyday of porcelain production under the Ming dynasty. It is exquisite in its perfection, its clarity and uniformity of line. The old patterns have been copied on a very large scale, and are now frequently found on a variety of everyday objects – vases, plates used for wall decoration, lamps, etc.

Snuff-boxes

Since Matteo Ricci brought the first snuff-box to the Emperor Wan Li in 1610 as a gift from the Pope, the Chinese have produced enormous numbers of such items in porcelain, jade, ivory and other materials. Old snuff-boxes fetch many thousand dollars, but present-day products can be had for as little as HK$40.

Specialized dealers

If you want to buy genuine antiques it is essential to go to an established and reputable firm. The following is a brief selection:

C. C. Tih Gallery
146–147 Prince's Building, 5 Ice House Street, Hong Kong
Open Mon.–Sat. 10 a.m.–6 p.m.

Charlotte Horstmann Ltd
104 Ocean Terminal, Kowloon
Open Mon.–Sat. 9.30 a.m.–6 p.m.
Also at Mandarin Hotel, Connaught Road, Hong Kong
Open Mon.–Sat. 9.30 a.m.–5.30 p.m.

Schoeni (Fine Oriental Art)
1 Hollywood Road, Hong Kong
Open Mon.–Sat. 9.30 a.m.–6 p.m.

P. C. Lu and Sons Ltd
Peninsula Hotel, Salisbury Road, Kowloon
Open Mon.–Sat. 9 a.m.–7 p.m., Sun. 9 a.m.–2 p.m.

Lane Crawford Antiques
Lane Crawford House, 70 Queen's Road Central, Hong Kong
Open Mon.–Fri. 9 a.m.–5.30 p.m., Sat. 9 a.m.–5 p.m.

Luen Chai
22 Upper Lascar Row, Hong Kong
Open daily 10 a.m.–6 p.m.

Four Treasures Art Gallery
1 Observatory Road (1st floor), Kowloon
Open daily 9 a.m.–6 p.m.

Netsuke House Ltd
159 Hollywood Road, Hong Kong
Open daily 10 a.m.–6 p.m.

The Antique House
11 Gran Avenida do Coronel Mesquita, Macau

Arrival

Exits from airport

There are three exits from Kai Tak Airport. The one to the right is for parties which are being met by special buses; cars from hotels pick up their passengers at the central exit (prior booking necessary); and passengers who want to use the airport bus or hire a taxi should follow the signs to the "Greeting Area". Local people meeting passengers usually wait at the left-hand exit.

Hotel reservations

Hotel rooms should be booked at least four weeks before leaving home. Help can be obtained from travel agencies, offices of the Hong Kong Tourist Association and the Portuguese Tourist Office (see Information) and airlines.
Passengers arriving in Hong Kong without a hotel reservation can apply to the hotel booking desk in the arrival hall after passing through the customs. Here transfers to Hong Kong and Kowloon can also be arranged.

Narcotics and drugs

Customs and baggage control officials in Hong Kong are almost exclusively concerned with the search for narcotics and are highly skilled in discovering hiding-places. All visitors should take care to be "clean" in this respect if they want to avoid going to jail. Possession of even the smallest quantity of any narcotic is liable to bring a stiff prison sentence.
See Airport and Boat travel.

Banks

Hong Kong has branches of banks from all over the world. Altogether 140 banks, with 1146 branches, are licensed to deal with the public, while 108 others are represented by agents. 302 finance companies, many of them subsidiaries of the banks, are registered in Hong Kong.

Some British and North American banks in Hong Kong:

American Express International Banking Corporation
Connaught Centre (28th floor), Hong Kong

Bank of America
12F Gloucester Tower, 11 Pedder Street, Hong Kong

Bank of Scotland
Connaught Centre, Hong Kong

Barclays Bank International
Connaught Centre (5th floor), Hong Kong

Chase Manhattan Bank
World Trade Centre, P.O. Box 104, Hong Kong
720 Nathan Road, Kowloon

Citibank
Citibank Tower, 8 Queen's Road Central, Hong Kong

Lloyds Bank International
2901–4 Admiralty Centre Tower, Harcourt Road, Hong Kong

Midland Bank
3802 Gloucester Tower, 11 Pedder Street, Hong Kong

Morgan Guaranty Trust Co. of New York
Alexandra House, 16–20 Chater Road Central, Hong Kong

National Westminster Bank
6F St George's Building, 2 Ice House Street, Hong Kong

Royal Bank of Canada
10 Ice House Street (12th floor), Hong Kong

Opening times

There are no standard opening times but as a general rule banks are open from 9.30 a.m. to 3 p.m. Monday to Friday, and from 9.30 to 12 on Saturday mornings.

Bureaux de change

Bureaux de change are mainly in Tsimshatsui, in the center of Kowloon, and near the big hotels on Hong Kong. They often offer better rates of exchange than the banks, and if you want to change large sums it is a good idea to compare the various rates. Licensed money-changers are authorized to display a sign to that effect.
Money can be changed on arrival at the airport but the rates are not so good, which makes it advisable to change enough before leaving home to cover paying out small sums such as tips, etc., on arrival.
See Currency.

Bathing beaches

The municipal authorities maintain and control 41 of the many beaches around the coasts of Hong Kong. Most of them have suitable amenities – kiosks, showers, toilets and changing rooms. Between May and October the average water temperature is about 27 °C/81 °F, during the rest of the year 19 °C/66 °F. Most people go to the beaches between about 9 a.m. and 6.30 p.m., but at weekends many young people spend the night there, to the accompaniment of music and barbecues. On the beaches run by the municipality there are lifeguards trained in first aid.
On sunny weekends the beaches – particularly those at Deep Water Bay, Repulse Bay, Shek O, Big Wave Bay and Stanley Beach – are overcrowded, and there are long queues for public transport.

Typhoon warning

During the typhoon season (June–Septenber) it is highly dangerous to go into the sea when a typhoon warning is in force, since the normally shallow surf gives place to heavy waves and the resultant undertow can carry off the strongest swimmer.

Naturist bathing

There are no naturist beaches; and to avoid offending Chinese susceptibilities bathers should always change in the huts or changing rooms provided.

Hong Kong

Big Wave Bay
Bus: 2 to Shau Kei Wan, then 9 to Shek O road-end and from there 10 minutes' walk to the beach.
The beach with the biggest waves.

Chung Hom Kok (between Repulse Bay and Stanley)
Bus: 6, 262.

Deep Water Bay (between Repulse Bay and Aberdeen)
Bus: 6 to Stanley, then 73.

Hair Pin
Bus: 6, 260 to Stanley.

Middle Bay
Bus: 6, 260 to Repulse Bay, then 10 minutes' walk.

Repulse Bay
See in A to Z section.

Shek O
Bus: 2 to Shau Kei Wan, then 9.

South Bay
Bus: 6, 260 to Repulse Bay, then 30 minutes' walk.

Stanley Main Beach
Bus: 6, 260 to Stanley.

New Territories (mainland)

Cafeteria (old), Cafeteria (new)
Casam, Castle Park, Lido, Ting Kau
Bus: 50. All from Jordan Road bus station, Kowloon.

Camper's
Bus: 5, 9 from Star Ferry bus station, Kowloon to Choi Hung bus station, then 92 to Pak Wai village and from there 20 minutes' walk.

Clear Water Bay
Bus: 5, 9 to Choi Hung bus station, then 91.

Hap Mun, Kiu Tsui and Pak Sha Chau
Bus: 5, 9 to Choi Hung bus station, then 92 to Sai Kung bus station, then sampan to beach.

Silverstrand
Bus: 5, 9 to Choi Hung bus station, then 91.

Trio
Bus: 5, 9 to Choi Hung bus station, then 92 to Pak Wai village and ferry to beach.

Cheung Chau

On the island of Cheung Chau (see A to Z section) there are two beaches, Kwun Yam Wan and Tung Wan.
Ferry from Outlying Districts Pier, Connaught Road, Hong Kong.

Lamma

There are two good beaches on the island of Lamma:

Hung Shing Yeh
Ferry to Yung Shu Wan (Lamma) from Outlying Districts Pier, Hong Kong.

Lo So Shing (West)
Ferry to Sok Kwu Wan (Lamma) from Outlying Districts Pier, Hong Kong.

Lantau

On the island of Lantau (see A to Z) there are three good beaches:

Cheung Shai and Pui O
Ferry from Outlying Districts Pier, Hong Kong, to Silvermine Bay.
Bus from ferry landing-stage (direction Pui O and Cheung Sha).
For Pui O beach get off in the centre of the village, then 10 minutes' walk.
These are Hong Kong's longest and finest beaches; uncrowded, particularly during the week.

Silvermine Bay
Ferry from Outlying Districts Pier, Hong Kong.

Macau

Baia de Lazaro

Ceoc Van

Hac Sa

See Macau A to Z, Coloane

See Swimming-pools.

Boat travel

Excursions

An interesting programme of cruises and excursions is offered by the firm of Watertours of Hong Kong, tel. 5–254808 and 3–686171. Reservations can be made either direct, in hotels, or through the Hong Kong Tourist Association (see Information). The colorful junks sail from the landing-stage between the Ocean Terminal and the Star Ferry Pier to Kowloon and from Blake Pier in Hong Kong. The trips last between 2 and $8\frac{1}{2}$ hours.

Cruise ships

Luxury passenger liners put in at the Ocean Terminal on their annual world cruises and other regular callers at Hong Kong are ships sailing various routes in Asia, as well as a few Soviet passenger ships. To get a berth on one of these vessels early reservation is necessary. Reservations can be made through travel agencies in Europe and North America.

Boutiques

In recent years the leading fashion houses of Europe and the United States have opened their own boutiques in Hong Kong. Although Hong Kong is the world's largest exporter of clothing, local products are rarely to be seen in the shops here.
Many firms have their boutiques in the shopping arcades of the large hotels; others have established themselves in the vicinity of the hotels.
Reasonably priced leisure clothing is sold by the following firms: Bang Bang, Michel René, Foxy Fashion, Wrangler, Join-In and Britannia, as well as in many small shops, where visitors will find the products of all the well-known manufacturers of jeans.

The following is a small selection of shops selling women's, men's and children's clothing.

Women's fashion

Adam and Eve
5 Ice House Street, Hong Kong
Open Mon.–Sat. 9.30 a.m.–6 p.m.

French Touch Ltd
Hilton Hotel, 1 Queen's Road Central, Hong Kong
Open Mon.–Sat. 9 a.m.–8 p.m., Sun. 10 a.m.–7 p.m.

Joyce Boutique
Mandarin Hotel Arcade, Connaught Road, Hong Kong
Open Mon.–Sat. 9 a.m.–6 p.m.

Peninsula Hotel, Salisbury Road, Kowloon
Open Mon.–Sat. 9 a.m.–6 p.m.

Jacques Furs
Lane Crawford Ltd, Lane Crawford House, Hong Kong
Open Mon.–Sat. 9 a.m.–6 p.m.

Gucci
Peninsula Hotel, Salisbury Road, Kowloon
Open Mon.–Sat. 10 a.m.–7 p.m.

Men's clothing

Ding How Department Store
Star House, Salisbury Road, Kowloon
Open daily 9.30 a.m.–1 a.m.

Gucci
Peninsula Hotel, Salisbury Road, Kowloon
Open Mon.–Sat. 10 a.m.–7 p.m.

Hermes
Peninsula Hotel, Salisbury Road, Kowloon
Open Mon.–Sat. 10 a.m.–6.30 p.m.

MacBeth
130–139 Prince's Building, 5 Ice House Street, Hong Kong
Open Mon.–Sat. 9.30 a.m.–6.30 p.m.

Children's clothing

Lane Crawford Ltd
Lane Crawford House, 70 Queen's Road Central, Hong Kong
Open Mon.–Sat. 9 a.m.–6 p.m.

Mother World
115 Ocean Terminal, Kowloon
Open daily 9.30 a.m.–7.30 p.m.

Little Things Ltd
31 Wellington Street, Hong Kong
Open Mon.–Fri. 9.30 a.m.–5.30 p.m., Sat. 9.30 a.m.–4 p.m.

See Shopping.

Business trips

It is particularly important on business trips to relate to the customs and mentality of the person you are dealing with.

Throughout Asia what counts is patience. Before getting down to business there has to be a certain amount of chatting in order to get to know something of the other person. Many Western business people often mistake for assent the Asian form of politeness that means one cannot directly contradict the other person, however cogent the reasons may be for doing so.
Considerable weight is attached to being properly dressed, and visiting-cards in English and Chinese are also essential. There are plenty of printers who specialize in that kind of job, and can turn them out very promptly. The major airlines also offer business travelers this service.

Camping

There are no campsites with the kind of facilities found on sites in Europe and North America; but many people spend the night in tents on the beaches at weekends and during the holiday season, or spend a few days camping on a site they have found for themselves in the New Territories or on one of the islands (particularly Lantau).

Campers should:
Remember to take enough water and food, maps and insect repellents.
Use care in lighting fires (danger of bush and forest fires).
Leave information about their whereabouts.
Take account of weather conditions (e.g. remember that during a typhoon warning, traffic comes to a halt).

Car rental

Hong Kong

Car rental firms mostly use Japanese vehicles, and in the luxury class Mercedes. Since Hong Kong's streets are almost permanently bottlenecked, visitors should consider whether it is not preferable to rely on taxis (which are cheap) or on public transport. See Motoring, Public transport.

With driver

Cars can also be rented with a driver. The price includes petrol and unlimited mileage.

Documents

To rent a car visitors must produce their national driving license and an international driving permit. Most firms will not hire to drivers under 25.

Car rental firms (a selection)

Avis, 85 Leighton Road, Hong Kong, tel. 5–719237

Wuhu Car Park Building, Dock Street, Hung Hom, Kowloon

Hertz, 102 Cayton House, 1 Duddell Street, Hong Kong

Macau

The only cars available for rental at the moment are jeep-type mini-mokes:

Macao Mokes Group Ltd.,
1st floor, Macao Ferry Terminal Building
tel. Macau 78851, Hong Kong 434190

Chemists

Chemists' shops in Hong Kong often follow the American drugstore model, selling perfume, toilet articles, stationery, toys, etc., as well as medicine.

Over-the-counter drugs

Most medicinal preparations are available without prescription, including antibiotics, the milder sedatives, pain-killers and contraceptive pills.

Watson's – The Chemist

The firm of Watson's – The Chemist has branches all over the city and in some hotels (Hilton, Sheraton, Hong Kong, and Repulse Bay Hotel). The largest branches are in Wheelock House, Hong Kong, and in the Ocean Centre and New World Centre in Kowloon.

Chinese medicine shops

In almost every part of the city visitors will find Chinese medicine shops which make and sell remedies prepared from plant and animal products in accordance with traditional recipes.

Church services

Protestant churches in Hong Kong

St John's Cathedral, Garden Road
Sun. at 9 a.m. and 11 a.m., Mon.–Sat. at 5 p.m.

Union Church, 22A Kennedy Road
Sun. at 10.30 a.m.

Christian Science Church, 31 Macdonnell Road
Sun. at 11 a.m., Wed. at 6 p.m.

Protestant churches in Kowloon

St Andrew's Church, 138 Nathan Road
Sun. at 11 a.m.

Christ Church, 132 Waterloo Road
Sun. at 10 a.m.

Emmanuel Church, 218 Nathan Road
Sun. at 11 a.m.

Roman Catholic churches in Hong Kong

Catholic Cathedral, 16 Caine Road
Masses daily every hour from 6 to 11 a.m., Sat. at 7 p.m.

Catholic Centre Chapel, 19 Connaught Road
Masses daily at 8 a.m. and 11 a.m., Sat. at 5.30 p.m.

St Joseph's Church, 7 Garden Road
Masses daily at 8, 9, 10, 11.30 a.m. and 6 p.m., Sat at 6 p.m.

Roman Catholic churches in Kowloon

St Francis of Assisi Church, 58 Shek Kip Mei Street
Masses daily every hour from 7 to 11 a.m., Sat. at 6 p.m.

St Mary's Church, 162 Austin Road
Masses daily every hour from 7 to 11 a.m., Sat. at 6.30 p.m.

Rosary Church, 125 Chatham Road
Masses daily every hour from 7 a.m. to noon, Sat. at 6 p.m.

Synagogue

Oheal Leah Synagogue, 70 Robinson Road, Hong Kong
Fri. at 6.30 p.m., Sat. at 9 a.m.

Clothing

Apart from the cooler winter months (January–March) there is no need to wear heavy warm clothing in Hong Kong. Because of the very hot and humid climate it's best to keep to light and washable cottons, although synthetic materials can also be worn from October to December. Dress is informal in the daytime although it is unusual to see men or women wearing shorts. Women visitors should try to avoid unduly low-cut blouses, etc. and men are expected to wear a collar and tie for business meetings or dining out in exclusive restaurants and the like.

Credit cards

Hotels, car rental firms, airlines, city-center restaurants and shops take all the major international credit cards, including

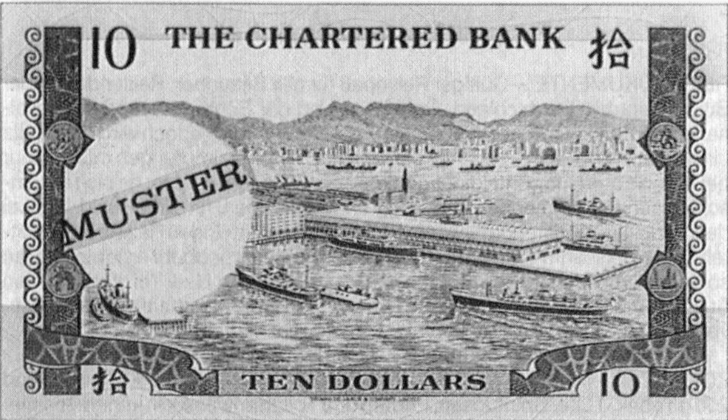

Hong Kong 10-dollar bill

American Express, Bank Americard (Visa), Carte Blanche, Diners Club, Master Card (Eurocard) and Overseas Trust Bank.
See Banks and Currency.

Currency

Hong Kong

The national currency is the Hong Kong dollar (HK$), which is divided into 100 cents. There are banknotes, issued by the Hongkong and Shanghai Banking Corporation and the Chartered Bank, for 10, 50, 100, 500 and 1000 dollars; each bank has its own design, but the colors of the various notes are the same. The government mints coins in denominations of 5, 10, 20 and 50 cents and 1, 2 and 5 dollars. The 1-cent notes, looking like toy money, are of more interest as souvenirs than as currency.
There are no restrictions on the import, purchase, sale or export of any currency.
When changing money it is a good idea to compare the conditions as well as the rates since many money-changers who offer a good rate may also charge 7 per cent commission, which cancels out the gain on the rate.
Before changing money back from Hong Kong dollars on departure make sure you keep some back to pay the airport tax.
See Airport and Banks.

Macau 100-pataca bill

Macau

The Macau pataca is made up of 100 avos. There are banknotes for 5, 10, 50, 100 and 500 patacas, and coins for 1, 5, 10, 20 and 50 avos.
There are no restrictions on the import or export of foreign currency. The Macau pataca is worth a few cents less than the Hong Kong dollar, which is freely negotiable in Macau, although the pataca cannot be used in Hong Kong. Money can be changed in the port.
It is advisable to reckon up what incidentals on the journey will cost then take about twice that amount in currency.
To be on the safe side, cash (preferably US dollars in small denominations) should be kept to a minimum. Traveler's cheques (also in US dollars) are much safer and are easier to replace in the event of loss. Many places such as hotels, restaurants and shops that get a number of foreign customers will also take internationally accepted credit cards (see entry) but because there are often considerable variations in the rate of exchange it is more difficult to judge in this instance how much you are actually spending.

Customs regulations

Hong Kong and Macau are free trade zones.

Hong Kong

Visitors may not, however, bring in duty-free more than 200 cigarettes or 50 cigars or 250 g of tobacco, 1 litre of spirits and a certain amount of perfume.
There is a ban in both Hong Kong and Macau on the import of weapons, explosives and drugs.

Macau

Macau has no other customs restrictions but anyone returning to Hong Kong from Macau should bear in mind that they will only be allowed to take in the quantities mentioned above (i.e. 200 cigarettes and 1 bottle of wine per person).

Department stores

There are two kinds of department store in Hong Kong – those run by the People's Republic of China and those based on Western models. The Chinese stores sell only goods produced in the People's Republic (e.g. quilted jackets, silk blouses, porcelain, carved ivory), which are not always of the highest quality but are nevertheless attractive and are certainly cheap. The Western-style stores stock goods from all over the world, but rarely local products. Some of these stores set their sights on the middle income ranges of the population; others are more up-market.
See also Shopping.

Chinese stores (a selection)

Chinese Arts and Crafts
3 Salisbury Road, Star House, Kowloon
Wyndham Street, Central, Hong Kong
Better-class Chinese products

Chung Kiu Chinese Arts and Crafts
Sai Yeung Choi Street, Kowloon
Better-class Chinese products

China Products Co.
488 Hennessy Road, Hong Kong

Chinese Merchandise Emporium
Chiao Shang Building
92–94 Queen's Road Central, Hong Kong

Yue Hwa Chinese Products Emporium Ltd
300–306 Nathan Road, Kowloon

Western-type stores (a selection)

Daimaru
Paterson Street, Causeway Bay, Hong Kong
Japanese-owned, with many European articles

Dragon Seed
39 Queen's Road Central, Hong Kong
Textiles, including top European and American brand names

Isetan
Shopping Mall, Sheraton Hotel, Kowloon
Japanese-owned, selling mainly European goods

Lane Crawford Ltd
70 Queen's Road Central, Hong Kong
Hong Kong's top quality shop

Matsuzakaya,
Paterson Street, Causeway Bay, Hong Kong
Japanese-owned

Shui Hing
23–25 Nathan Road, Kowloon
Open daily 10 a.m.–8 p.m.

Sincere Department Store
173 Des Voeux Road Central, Hong Kong
Open Mon.–Sat. 10 a.m.–6.30 p.m.

Wing On Co. Ltd
211 Des Voeux Road Central, Hong Kong
Open Mon.–Sat. 10 a.m.–6.30 p.m.
361 Nathan Road, Kowloon
Open Tues.–Sun. 11 a.m.–9.30 p.m., closed Mon.

Diplomatic missions

United Kingdom

British Trade Commission
Bank of America Tower (9th floor)
12 Harcourt Road, Hong Kong
tel. 5–230176

Canada

Asian House (14th–15th floors)
1 Hennessy Road, Hong Kong
tel. 5–282222
Open weekdays 8.30–11 a.m.

Australia

Connaught Centre (11th floor)
Connaught Road Central, Hong Kong
tel. 5–227171
Open weekdays 9.30 a.m.–noon, and 1–4 p.m.

New Zealand

3414 Connaught Centre
Connaught Road Central, Hong Kong
tel. 5–255044
Open weekdays 9 a.m.–1 p.m. and 2–5.30 p.m.

United States

26 Garden Road, Hong Kong
tel. 5–239011
Open weekdays (except Wed.) 8.30 a.m.–noon; Wed. 8.30–10.30 a.m.

Doctors

By law doctors are not allowed to advertise; but visitors who need a doctor can obtain names and addresses from their national diplomatic mission.

Public hospitals

Kowloon
Princess Margaret Hospital
Lui King Hill Road, Laichikok
tel. 3–7427111

Queen Elizabeth Hospital
Wylie Road, Kowloon
tel. 3–7102111

Hong Kong Island
Queen Mary Hospital
Pokfulam Road
tel. 5–8192111

Tang Shiu Kin Hospital
Queen's Road East
tel. 5–742331

Private hospitals

Kowloon
St Theresa's Hospital
327 Prince Edward Road
tel. 3–7119111

Baptist Hospital
222 Waterloo Road
tel. 3–374141

Hong Kong Island
Hong Kong Adventist Hospital
40 Stubbs Road
tel. 5–746211

Canossa Hospital
1 Old Peak Road
tel. 5–222181

Electricity

Hong Kong

200–230 volts A.C., 50 cycles. Appliances designed for 220 volts can be operated without difficulty on 200 volts. Hotel bathrooms have universal sockets for razors, etc. but hair dryers and heated rollers often require special adapters. These can be obtained from the big hotels and electrical shops.

Macau

The newer parts of Macau have 220 volts and 50 cycles, but in the older section the electricity is 110 volts and 50 cycles.

Emergency calls

For police, fire or medical emergency dial 999. The exchange will then connect you with the service required.

Events

The exact dates of regular annual events may vary from year to year, and there are also film festivals, sporting occasions and street festivals which take place at irregular intervals. The Hong Kong Tourist Association (see Information) publishes an up-to-date list of events every year, and the City Hall (tel. 5–229928), the Hong Kong Arts Centre (tel. 5–271122) and the Hong Kong Tourist Information Service (tel. 3–671111) produce monthly calendars of events.
Further information can be obtained from the television periodical "TV and Entertainment Times", the local radio station RTHK 4 (daily at 7.45 a.m.) and the English-language television channel (on Fridays after the main news bulletin and weather forecast). The radio and television programmes are called "What's On".

January

Hong Kong Ready-to-Wear Festival
Chinese New Year Celebrations
Asia–Pacific Orienteering Championship

February

Hong Kong Arts Festival
Hong Kong Open Golf Championship
Lantern Festival, Macau

March

Yuen Siu (Lantern Festival)
Hong Kong Arts Festival
Hong Kong Ladies Amateur Open Golf Championship
Urban Council Flower Show
Hong Kong International Film Festival
Hong Kong Schools Music Festival

April

Ching Ming Festival (like Easter)
Arts Festival for the disabled, Bonsai Show

May

Birthday of Tin Hau (Hong Kong) and Festival of A Ma (Macau), patroness of seafarers
Cheung Chau Bun Festival

	Asian Amateur Singing Contest Miss Hong Kong Pageant Asian Antiques Fair End of the horse-racing season
June	Tuen Ng (Dragon Boat Festival) with international dragon boat races
August	Yue Lan, Hungry Ghost Festival Maiden's Festival Hong Kong Open Junior Gold Championship
September	Hong Kong Jewelery and Watch Fair Mid-Autumn Festival Start of the horse-racing season
October	Chung Yeung Festival Asian Arts Festival
November	Macau Grand Prix Macau International Marathon Hong Kong International Go-Kart Grand Prix Seiko Super Tennis Hong Kong Amateur Cross-Harbour Swimming Race
December	Hong Kong International Salon of Photography Flying Fifteen World Championship

See also Folk traditions, Public holidays and Festivals.

Ferries

Hong Kong Star Ferry

This ferry – made famous by the movie "Love is a Many Splendored Thing" – has been plying between Hong Kong Island (Central District) and Kowloon (Tsimshatsui) since 1880, and is one of the most spectacular and cheapest ferry rides in the world. Daily about every 5 minutes from 6.30 a.m. to 11.30 p.m. The crossing takes 10–15 minutes.

Hong Kong and Yaumatei Ferry

Hong Kong and Yaumatei Ferries (HYF) run services (foot passengers and car ferries) to Hong Kong's beautiful outer islands. There are ferries daily from 6.20 a.m. to 2 a.m. from the Outlying Islands Pier in Hong Kong Island's Central District about a half-mile walk west of Star Ferry Pier, from Wan Chai, North Point, or Shan Kei Wan to landing-stages in Kowloon and the New Territories at points such as Yaumatei, Sham Shui Poi, Hum Hom, Kwun Tong, Tuen Min and Tsing Yi. Hydrofoils run up the Pearl River to Canton (Guangzhou). A bit farther west of Star Ferry Pier ferries leave from the ocean liner terminals at half-hourly or hourly intervals for the islands of Lantau, Lamma, Cheung Chau and Peng Chau on a pleasant crossing which takes 45–90 minutes. All the ferries only operate until 10–11.30 p.m.
Information from the Hong Kong and Yaumatei Ferry Company, tel. 5–423081.
It is advisable to buy a return ticket and get to the pier 10–15 minutes before departure time since the ferries become very crowded, especially on public holidays and at weekends.

Star Ferry Pier, the link between Hong Kong and Kowloon

Macau

Four firms operate ferry services making the 40-mile trip from Hong Kong to Macau:

Far East Hydrofoil Company (conventional ferries and jetfoils)
Shun Tak Centre Terminal, Connaught Road Central, Hong Kong (tel. 5-457021)

Hong Kong Macau Hydrofoil Company Ltd (jetcats and hydrofoils)
New World Tower (33rd floor), 16–18 Queen's Road Central, Hong Kong (tel. 5–218302)

Sealink Ferries Ltd (hoverferries)
Central Harbour Services Pier, Pier Road, Central, Hong Kong (tel. 5-423081)

Hong Kong Hi-Speed Ferries Ltd
Hong Kong and Macau Wharf Terminal, Connaught Road Central, Hong Kong (tel. 5–8152299)

Departures from Shun Tak Terminal (Hong Kong Island) and Shamshuipo (Kowloon). There is a departure tax (about HK$8) from Hong Kong, none from Macau.

Bookings should be made in good time, especially at weekends and in the vacation season. Telephone bookings are possible for hydrofoils and jetcats only (tel. 5–232136, from 8 a.m. to 8 p.m.).

Conventional ferries:
6 round trips daily, crossing takes about 3 hours.

Hi-Speed ferries:
7 services daily (8 a.m.–11 p.m.), crossing takes about $1\frac{1}{2}$ hours.

Hoverferries:
8 services daily (8 a.m.–5 or 6 p.m.), crossing takes about 70 minutes.

Hydrofoils:
22 round trips daily (8 a.m.–5 or 6 p.m.), crossing takes about 75 minutes.

Jetcats (jet-propelled catamarans):
10 round trips daily, crossing takes about 75 minutes.

Jetfoils:
Every half-hour daily from 7 a.m. to 1.30 a.m., crossing takes about 55 minutes.

Wallah-wallahs

From dawn onwards little "wallah-wallah" boats ply around the harbor. They are busiest in the evenings when the Star Ferry has finished for the day and ships' personnel want to get back on board, but have become less important with the advent of the MTR and the Cross-Harbour Tunnel.

Fitness centers

Many hotels have fitness centers, with sauna baths and massage as well as, in some cases, jacuzzies, tennis courts and squash courts.

Hong Kong Island

Furama International
1 Connaught Road Central, tel. 5–255111

Hong Kong Hilton
2 Queen's Road Central, tel. 5–233111

The Mandarin
5 Connaught Road Central, tel. 5–220111

Harbour
116–122 Gloucester Road, tel. 5–748211

Park Lane
310 Gloucester Road, tel. 5–7901021

Kowloon

Holiday Inn Golden Mile
46–52 Nathan Road, tel. 3–693111

Holiday Inn Harbour View
70 Mody Road, tel. 3–7215161

The Hongkong
3 Canton Road, tel. 3–676011

Miramar
134 Nathan Road, tel. 3–681111

Regal Meridian
71 Mody Road, tel. 3–7221818

The Royal Garden
69 Mody Road, tel. 3–7215215

Shangri-La
64 Mody Road, tel. 3–7212111

Sheraton
20 Nathan Road, tel. 3–691111

Macau

Estoril
6 Ave. Sidonio Pais, tel. 572081–3

The Oriental
Ave. da Amizade, tel. 567888

Hyatt Regency
Taipa Island, tel. 27000

Lisboa
Ave. da Amizade, tel. 77666

Presidente
Ave. da Amizade, tel. 71822

Sintra
Ave. da Amizade, tel. 85111

See Sport.

Folk traditions

Arts Festival, Festival of Asian Arts

Chinese folk traditions and folk art are displayed in performances given during the Hong Kong Arts Festival and the Festival of Asian Arts, which are held every year (see Events). The municipal authorities also give local artists and performers opportunities throughout the year of displaying their skills either in the City Hall or in the open air in parks and residential areas.

Hong Kong Arts Centre

The Hong Kong Arts Centre also has a regular program of performances and events. Visitors should not miss the opportunity of seeing a performance of a Cantonese opera; and among other attractive entertainments there are concerts of Chinese classical music, puppet plays, recitals of folk-songs, demonstrations of the famous sword dance and performances of Chinese plays.

Information

Information about programs can be obtained from the City Hall (tel. 5–229928) and the Hong Kong Arts Centre (tel. 5–271122).
See Events, Public holidays and Festivals.

Food and drink

Food

Confucius said "enjoying your food is the first among pleasures", and the Chinese enter into the spirit of this by making a feast of every meal. They take their time over their food and really relish it, putting body and soul into it, with nearly always the whole family taking part.

Eating with chopsticks

In East Asia most meals are eaten with chopsticks, and it is a good idea for Europeans to try and eat with chopsticks as well. You can soon acquire the necessary manual dexterity in practice, and surprising as it may seem food actually tastes different when eaten with chopsticks. There is a simple explanation for this. With a fork you scoop up quite large

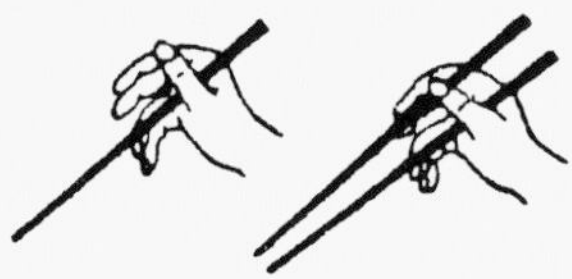

mouthfuls and this generally means that the various components of a dish all get eaten together at the same time. However with chopsticks you can only pick up small amounts at a time, so you get to savor every morsel individually. This effect is heightened by the fact that Chinese cooking pays special attention in its preparation to maintaining or even intensifying the special nature of each ingredient.
Chopsticks come in a wide variety of materials ranging from plain bamboo to those that have been ornately lacquered or carved out of ivory. You should hold the chopsticks in your right hand, with the lower one lying in the hollow between the thumb and the forefinger, resting on the "ring" finger next to the little finger, while holding the upper one between the thumb, forefinger and middle finger so that it is easy to manipulate into position.
A host will always seat his guest with his face to the door, while he himself sits with his back to it. It is regarded as a courteous gesture for the host to help his guest, or a friend, or his wife, to food from the dish, transferring it to the other person's bowl either with a special pair of chopsticks or with his own chopsticks turned the other way round.

Hong Kong

In Hong Kong one can run through the whole gamut of Chinese cooking. There are regional specialties from Chiu Chow, Shanghai, Peking, Szechuan, etc., but the most popular of all is Canton where most of the Crown Colony's inhabitants come from. No fewer than 30,000 of Hong Kong's restaurants and eating-houses serve this region's mild and infinitely varied dishes. Chinese meals are considerably cheaper than corresponding Western-style menus. The following sections give some idea of the specialties from the various regions.

Canton

The basic elements of Cantonese cooking are rice, chicken and pork, along with fish and seafood. Its dishes are moist rather than dry, always freshly prepared and may contain ingredients that seem rather strange to many European palates, although

A Chinese meal – eaten with chopsticks

there is nothing problematic about such specialties as sliced beef with oyster sauce, sweet and sour pork, clear mushroom soup, minced chicken with corn soup and stuffed crab claw. However, most people will balk at such odd items as goosefeet, sea cucumbers or even dog (which is legally banned in Hong Kong in any case, although it is permitted in nearby Macau). Meals are accompanied by bread or boiled or fried rice, and soup comes at the end of the meal, not the beginning. The common condiments are soya sauce, vinegar and chili sauce, while the usual drink with the meal is tea, though most restaurants also have beer, wine, etc.

Chiu Chow

Chiu Chow specialties include Chiu Chow soya goose, shark's fin soup (served with ginger, chicken broth and soya sauce), stewed pig's shanks, fried Chiujew chicken and fried oysters with scrambled egg. The most famous of all Chiu Chow specialties, however, is bird's nest soup, made from the saliva-glue of nesting swifts added to a basic chicken stock. See Restaurants.

Peking

Peking Chinese restaurants are much fewer and far between than those serving Cantonese food. Peking cuisine from the colder northern Chinese regions is designed to be filling and warming, and is heavily spiced, often serving noodles instead of rice. Peking duck (kwa lo aap) is a famous northern delicacy which stretches over three courses, including the duck's crisply roast skin wrapped in a kind of wheat pancake (bao bing), and seasoned with spring onions and a special sauce. The rest of the duck, apart from the flesh, which provides the second course, is used to make a soup. This is a very filling dish, easily enough for four people, and should be ordered in advance. The same is true of "Beggar's Chicken" in which the bird is stuffed, seasoned, wrapped in lotus leaves and baked in hot ashes in a clay covering. Cracking the clay open with a hammer is quite a ceremony in itself. Other typical Northern dishes are diced chicken and walnuts, spiced beef with quick-fried shrimps, shredded pork with green peppers and ziao zi, little ravioli-like pasta envelopes filled with steamed or fried fish. Mongolian hotpot (ta pin lo) is especially popular in Peking restaurants during the winter months. This is made fondu-style in a chafing-dish set in the center of the table, filled with boiling water or soup stock into which you dip thin slices of raw meat or fish which, when cooked, are eaten with a specially prepared sauce. You can then drink the broth. See Restaurants.

Shanghai

Shanghai specialties include fried eel with soya sauce, shrimps with green peas, meat balls with vegetables, sliced beef with green chili and fried crab. The dishes are even more heavily spiced than those from Peking. See Restaurants.

Szechuan

Dishes from this region, which are also very popular with people who enjoy spiced food, include shredded pork with garlic sauce, sweet and sour fish, fried spicy shrimp, marinated duck and lettuce with chicken. See Restaurants.

Dim Sum

"Yum Xha" is a very popular institution in Hong Kong and involves enjoying the famous Cantonese daytime snacks known as Dim Sum, washed down with great quantities of tea. There are about 2000 of these delicious little snacks and savouries in the Cantonese repertoire, the best known being shiu mai (steamed minced pork and shrimp dumpling), chun kuen (deep-fried spring roll with a savoury filling) and ha gau (steamed shrimp dumpling). They are usually served up on trays or in bamboo baskets from which you can take your pick. Desserts worth trying are boiled water chestnuts (ma tai go) or rice pudding (sai mai). See Restaurants.
For Western dishes, other Asian specialties, etc., see Restaurants.

Macau

Anyone who want a change from Hong Kong's predominantly Chinese cooking should find Macau a real oasis, where Western cooking is mainly represented in the form of simple Portuguese dishes. Fish, meat and poultry are usually accompanied by tomatoes, potatoes and small black olives. Many dishes are steamed, including lobster which is remarkably tasty prepared in this way. Fish and seafood are generally excellent, and distinctly cheaper than in Hong Kong. Portugual's African colonies were the source of "African Chicken" in which the bird is grilled and spiced with exotic ingredients. The wine is first class, both red and white, and better value than in Hong Kong, and Macau also has excellent port.

Drink

Most Chinese only drink tea with their meals. The most popular alcoholic drinks are beer, whisky, cognac or rice wine (shao xing or mao tai) which is generally drunk warm. "Hua Diao" is the best-known brand of rice wine, though "Jia Fan" is better and less expensive. Virtually any of the world's beers and spirits can be obtained in Hong Kong. The most popular locally brewed beers are "San Miguel" and "Löwenbräu", while Carlsberg is also an imported favorite. The Chinese beer from the former German colony of Tsingtau is much cheaper than that imported from the West.

Galleries

Chinese art

Yub Tai Choon Ltd
270 and 274 Queen's Road Central, Hong Kong
Open Mon.–Sat. 9.30 a.m.–6 p.m.
Of special interest: Chinese fans

Pok Art House
18 Granville Road, Kowloon
Open Mon.–Sat. 10 a.m.–7 p.m., Sun. 1–6 p.m.
Of special interest: Chinese paintings.

Tsi Ku Chai
South China Building (1st floor)
1 Wyndham Street, Hong Kong
Open Mon.–Sat. 10 a.m.–6 p.m.
Of special interest: Chinese calligraphy

Western art

Galerie du Monde
Hollywood Commercial House (2nd floor)
3–5 Old Bailey Street, Hong Kong
Open Mon.–Sat. 9 a.m.–6 p.m.
Of special interest: contemporary graphic art

Art East Art West
Petra Hinterhür
8 Plunkett's Road, 13 Strawberry Hill, Hong Kong
Open by appointment

Pao Sui Loon Galleries
See Hong Kong A–Z, Pao Sui Loon.

Getting to Hong Kong

By air

Most visitors to Hong Kong travel by air, and it is in fact the center of civil air transport in Asia. Thirty-four international airlines have scheduled direct flights to Hong Kong (sometimes with stopovers), from cities such as Amsterdam, Frankfurt, Geneva, London, Paris, Zürich, Rome, etc. All of Asia's major airports can be reached by direct connections. Since Macau has no airport of its own it is best to travel there via Hong Kong.
See Airlines
See Airport
See Air travel

By sea

Most vessels berth in Hong Kong's Middle Harbour but the big passenger liners usually dock at the Ocean Terminal in Kowloon's shopping district of Tsimshatsui. Ferryboats, hydrofoils, hovercraft, etc. maintain a frequent service between Hong Kong and Macau. For up-to-date timetables see the daily press. Crossings by boat take considerably longer ($2\frac{1}{2}$ hours) than by hydrofoil or hovercraft, but are far more restful. The fastest crossing is by jetfoil, which takes 45–55 minutes. Hydrofoils and jetcats are not much slower, and only take about 70 minutes. These all leave from the new Macau Terminal in Victoria Harbour on Hong Kong Island, while the hovercraft, which take about an hour, and the hydrofoils, which only operate in the daytime, leave from Shamshuipo, Kowloon. It can be awkward and time-consuming to try and reserve a seat on a crossing since the ferries get very crowded, especially at weekends, so it is best to get tickets from a travel agent. Return trips by jetfoil can be booked, using a computer system, up to 28 days in advance. The most convenient booking terminals for tourists are in the MTR Stations in Central and Tsimshatsui, and in the New World Centre at Kowloon. Further information can be obtained by telephoning 5457021 in Hong Kong, 3677747 in Kowloon, and 573586 in Macau.

See Ferries
See Boat travel

By rail and by road

Hong Kong has only one railroad line, from Hung Hom Station in Kowloon to Canton, the provincial capital in the People's Republic of China.

It is possible to travel to the Far East from Europe overland by road or by rail but this will be out of the question for most people since it is fraught with all kinds of difficulty, but anyone with a nostalgic love of rail travel might like to know about the de-luxe train-trip overland to China by Central Kingdom Express, a 40-day tour run by Voyages Jules Verne (10 Glentworth Street, London NW1, tel. 4868751–3), with monthly departures throughout the summer, traveling from London (Victoria) via Paris, Warsaw, Moscow, the Trans-Siberian Railway, Irkutsh, Lake Baikal, Ulan Bator, Dalong, Peking, Xian, Kuoyang, Nanking, Shanghai and Canton to Hong Kong (Kowloon), with 1–3 day stopovers *en route* for sightseeing.

See Rail travel
See Railway stations

Health

The tropical climate, unaccustomed food and drink, jet-lag and the like can combine to make you feel a bit off-color. In the early days it is a good idea to avoid physical exertion and too much exposure to the sun, and also basically steer clear of raw food, peeled fruit, ice cream and tapwater. Cleanliness is the best protection against falling sick, i.e. keep on washing your hands, taking showers and changing your underwear. Your traveling medical kit will assume much more importance than it does in Europe, because there is a greater risk of infection and lots of medicines are either available in Asia under a completely different name, or not to be had at all. Obviously you need to take plentiful supplies of anything being prescribed for you at the time (including contraceptives), but it also pays to take your own thermometer, scissors, tweezers, cotton wool, bandages, plasters, antiseptic cream, painkillers, treatment for stomach upsets, travel sickness, sunburn, and barrier creams, etc.

See Chemists and Doctors.

Hospitals

See Doctors.

Hotels

Hong Kong

The following list is a selection of hotels and reasonably-priced guest-houses classified according to the price of a single room for one night:

A=US$90 plus B=US$60–90
C=US$40–60 D=US$35–40
SP: swimming-pool TV: television

The price of a double room is about 25 per cent more. There is usually also a service charge of 10 per cent, with taxes adding a further 4 per cent.

Hong Kong's hotels are the best in Asia, and some of them among the best in the world. They nearly all have air conditioning, and a telephone, color TV and refrigerator in every room. Since Hong Kong's hotels tend to get booked to capacity reservations need to be made well in advance. The Hong Kong Hotel Association's room reservation service at Kai Ta Airport can help with finding overnight accommodation if necessary.

Hotels

*Mandarin (A; TV)
5 Connaught Road Central, Hong Kong, tel. 5–220111

The Mandarin, one of Hong Kong's luxury hotels

Furamara (B; TV)
1 Connaught Road Central, Hong Kong, tel. 5–255111

Lee Gardens (B; TV)
Hysan Avenue, Causeway Bay, Hong Kong, tel. 5–767211

Excelsior (B; TV)
281 Gloucester Road, Causeway Bay, Hong Kong
tel. 5–757365

Hong Kong Hilton International (B; TV, SP)
2 Queen's Road Central, Hong Kong, tel. 5–233111

Park Lane (C; TV)
310 Gloucester Road, Causeway Bay, Hong Kong
tel. 5–7901021

Caravelle (C; TV)
84–86 Morrison Hill Road, Hong Kong, tel. 5–754455

Singapore (C; TV)
41–49 Hennessy Road, Hong Kong, tel. 5–272721

Cathy (D; TV)
17 Tung Lo Wan Road, Causeway Bay, Hong Kong
tel. 5–778211

Harbour (D; TV)
116–122 Gloucester Road, Hong Kong, tel. 5–748211

Luk Kwok (D; TV)
67 Gloucester Road, Hong Kong, tel. 5–270721

Guest houses

YMCA Headquarter Hostel (D; TV)
1 Macdonnell Road, Hong Kong, tel. 5–223101

Sailors' and Soldiers' Home (D)
22 Hennessy Road, Wanchai

Kowloon
Hotels

*Peninsula (A; TV)
Salisbury Road, Kowloon, tel. 3–666251

*Regent (A; TV, SP)
Salisbury Road, Kowloon, tel. 3–7211211

*Shangri-La (A; TV, SP)
64 Mody Road, East Tsimshatsui, Kowloon, tel. 3–7215215

*Prince (A; TV, SP)
Harbour City, Canton Road, Kowloon, tel. 3–7237788

*Hong Kong (A; TV, SP)
3 Canton Road, Kowloon, tel. 3–676011

Sheraton-Hong Kong (B; TV, SP)
20 Nathan Road, Kowloon, tel. 3–691111

Golden Mile Holiday Inn (B; TV, SP)
46–52 Nathan Road, Kowloon, tel. 3–693111

Harbour View Holiday Inn (B; TV, SP)
70 Mody Road, East Tsimshatsui, Kowloon, tel. 3–7215161

Hyatt Regency (B; TV)
67 Nathan Road, Kowloon, tel. 3–662321

Marco Polo (B; TV)
Harbour City, Canton Road, Kowloon, tel. 3–7215111

Miramar (B; TV)
134 Nathan Road, Kowloon, tel. 3–681111

Regal Meridian Hong Kong (B; TV)
71 Mody Road, East Tsimshatsui, Kowloon, tel. 3–7221818

Royal Garden (B; TV)
69 Mody Road, East Tsimshatsui, Kowloon, tel. 3–7215215

Ambassador (C; TV)
Nathan/Middle Roads, Kowloon, tel. 3–666321

New World (C; TV, SP)
22 Salisbury Road, East Tsimshatsui, Kowloon, tel. 3–694111

Regal Meridian Airport (C; TV)
Sa Po Road, Kowloon, tel. 3–7180333

Carlton (C; TV, SP)
$4\frac{1}{2}$ miles, Tai Po Road, Kowloon, tel. 3–866222

Fortuna (C; TV)
355 Nathan Road, Kowloon, tel. 3–851011

Grand (C; TV)
14 Carnarvon Road, Kowloon, tel. 3–669331

Imperial (C; TV)
30–34 Nathan Road, Kowloon, tel. 3–662201

Astor (D; TV)
11 Carnarvon Road, Kowloon, tel. 3–667261

Bangkok (D; TV)
2–12 Pilkem Street, Yaumati, Kowloon, tel. 3–679181

Chung Hing (D; TV)
380 Nathan Road, Kowloon, tel. 3–887001

Empress (D; TV)
17–19 Chatham Road, Kowloon, tel. 3–660211

Fortuna Court (D; TV)
3–5 Chi Wo Street, Kowloon, tel. 3–304321

Galaxie (D; TV)
30 Pak Hoi Street, Kowloon, tel. 3–307211

International (D; TV)
33 Cameron Road, Kowloon, tel. 3–663381

King's (D; TV)
473–473A Nathan Road, Kowloon, tel. 3–301281

Nathan (D; TV)
378 Nathan Road, Kowloon, tel. 3–885141

Ritz (D)
122 Austin Road, Kowloon, tel. 3–692282

Guest houses

Caritas Bianchi Lodge (D)
4 Cliff Road, Yaumati, Kowloon, tel. 3–881111

Chung King (D)
A block, 4th and 5th floors, 40 Nathan Road, Kowloon
tel. 3–665362–6

First Hotel (D)
206 Portland Street, Kowloon, tel. 3–305211–7

YMCA (D; TV, SP)
Salisbury Road, Kowloon, tel. 3–692211

YMCA International (D; TV)
23 Waterloo Road, Kowloon, tel. 3–319111

YMCA Anne Black Centre (D; TV)
5 Man Fuk Road, Waterloo Hill, Kowloon, tel. 3–7139211

See Youth hostels.

Macau

In the past Macau's hotel industry was thought to be rather underdeveloped, and capacity tended to be overestimated in the peak holiday season. Nowadays probably the most charming of Macau's hotels is the Pousada da São Tiago, picturesquely located in Barra Fort (see Macau A to Z, Fortaleza da Barra). The Hyatt Regency, with its own shuttle service, has recently opened on Taipa. On the mainland the new Oriental and the President stand beside the Outer Harbour, while behind them you have the Royal Hotel, on the other side of the hill and opposite Vasco da Gama Park. Other modern hotels include the Lisboa with its idiosyncratic architecture, the Estoril and the Matsuya. The Central, which is older but has recently been renovated, is a pleasant hotel, as is the Bela Vista.
Cheaper accommodation can be had at the Hoi Pan, Tai Fat or Universal. Coloane has the Pousada de Coloane, which is modern, clean and pleasantly quiet.
Macau tends to be cheaper than Hong Kong, and this also applies to the cost of a hotel. Bookings can be made in Hong Kong at the Macau Tourist Information Board, or you can phone direct to the hotel of your choice. It's a good idea to make a reservation early for the weekend since that is when people flock over from Hong Kong.
The following list is a selection of hotels and other accommodation, classified according to the price of a single room for one night:

A=US$90 plus	B=US$60–90
C=US$40–60	D=US$35–40
SP: swimming-pool	TV: television

The price of a double room is about 25 per cent more and there is also a 10 per cent service charge and taxes of 5 per cent.

Hotels

*Macau Oriental (A; TV, SP)
Ave. da Amizade, Macau, tel. M–567888

*Hyatt Regency (A; TV, SP)
Taipa Island, P.O. Box 3008, Central, Macau, tel. M–27000

Pousada de Sao Tiago (B; TV, SP)
Ave. da Republica, Macau, tel. M–78111

Presidente (C; TV)
Ave. da Amizade, Macau, tel. M–553888, 71822

Royal (C; TV, SP)
Estrada da Vitoria, Macau, tel. M–552222

Lisboa (C; TV, SP)
Ave. da Amizada, Macau, tel. M–77666

Sintra (C; TV)
Ave. D. Joao IV, Macau, tel. M–85111

Estoril (D)
Ave. Sidonio Pais, Macau, tel. M–57081–3

Pousada de Coloane (D; TV, SP)
Praia de Cheok Van, Coloane Island
tel. M–28144, HK–455626

Bela Vista (D)
8 Rue Comendador Kou Ho Neng, Macau, tel. M–573821

Central (D)
Ave. Almeida Ribeiro, Macau, tel. M–777000

London (D)
Praça Ponte e Horta, Macau, tel. M–83388

Man Va (D)
Rua da Caldeira, nos. 30–34, 3rd–5th floors, Macau
tel. M–88655–6

Matsuya (D)
5 Calçada de S. Francisco, Macau, tel. M–75466

Metropole (D)
63–63A Rua da Praia Grande, Macau, tel. M–88166

Mondial (D; TV)
Rua de Antonio Basto, Macau, tel. M–566866, 76498

Guest houses

Hoi Pan, 8 Travessa D. Afonso Henriques, Macau

Lao Lai, 65 Ave. Infante D. Henrique, 2nd floor.

Ka Va, Calçada de Sao Jose

Oceane, 2 Ave. Dr. Rodrigo Rodrigues, 1st floor

Tai Fat, 41–43 Rua de Felicidade, 2nd floor

Universal, 73 Rua de Felicidade, ground floor

Va Lai, 44 Rua da Praia Grande, 1st floor

See Youth hostels.

How to behave

Visitors should respect the feelings of the host population and behave in a discreet way so as not to cause "loss of face", which is seemingly the most dishonorable thing that can happen in Asia. You should try to avoid gesticulating as you speak since body language means more to an Asian than a European and many gestures that are thought quite innocuous in Europe have a distinct – and possibly obscene – significance in Asia. For example, you shouldn't clap anyone on the shoulder since that brings bad luck and can even mean a miscarriage for a pregnant woman. Don't take photographs of Buddhas or of Chinese praying to Buddha and lighting joss-sticks. This is considered disrespectful. Don't smoke in public transport or drop litter in the street – you can be fined up to HK$200. You can make local phone calls in Hong Kong from shops or cafés free of charge if you ask politely. You can spend hours looking around shops and trying things on without buying anything. There are few public toilets, and it's easier to go to the nearest hotel or restaurant. Visits to friends and acquaintances should be made from 8 to 8.30 in the evening onwards. It is customary to take fruit and cigarettes if invited out to someone's home, and if there are children there take them chocolate or biscuits. See Business trips.

Information

Hong Kong
The Hong Kong Tourist Association can supply a wide range of literature and maps covering such subjects as exciting things to do in Hong Kong, Chinese food, sightseeing, arts and crafts, shopping, Chinese festivals, museums, beaches, walks, the outlying islands, Ocean Park and public transport. These are readily available in the Association's Information Centres in Hong Kong.

In the United Kingdom

Apply for information to:
Hong Kong Tourist Association
14–16 Cockspur Street
London SW1Y 5DP
tel. (01) 930 4775

In the United States

Hong Kong Tourist Association
339 North Michigan Avenue
Chicago, IL 60601
tel. (312) 782 3872

Hong Kong Tourist Association
548 Fifth Avenue
New York, NY 10036
tel. (212) 947 5008

In Australia

Hong Kong Tourist Association
Bligh House, 4–6 Bligh Street
Sydney, NSW
tel. 232 2422

In New Zealand

Hong Kong Tourist Association
29–31 Shortland Street
P.O. Box 2120, Auckland
tel. 798642

In Hong Kong

Hong Kong Tourist Association

Kai Tak Airport
Buffer Hall
8 a.m.–11.30 p.m. daily, tel. 7697970

Star Ferry Concourse, Kowloon
Mon.–Fri. 8 a.m.–6 p.m.
Sat., Sun. 8 a.m.–1 p.m.

35th floor, Connaught Centre, Hong Kong Island
Mon.–Fri. 8 a.m.–6 p.m., tel. 5–244191

G8 Empire Centre, 68 Mody Road, East Tsimshatsui, Kowloon
daily 9 a.m.–7.30 p.m.

Government Publications Centre
General Post Office Building, Hong Kong

World Trade Centre
Causeway Bay, Hong Kong

Telephone information service during normal office hours: dial 3–7225555.

Information can also be obtained in hotels.

Tourist police, tel. 5–290000

Macau

In Hong Kong

Macau Tourist Information Bureau
1729 Star House, Salisbury Road
Tsimshatsui, Kowloon (next to the Star Ferry Pier)

In Macau

Department of Tourism
1 Travesso do Paiva, Macau
tel. 77218 (stand at the arrival wharf)

People's Republic of China

China Travel Service
77 Queen's Road Central, Hong Kong
tel. 5–259121

See Diplomatic missions.

Language

Hong Kong

Chinese is spoken by more people than any other language. It reflects the history and culture of a very ancient nation, with every character representing not letters but names, objects or concepts. It is written with great care since calligraphy is an art that is very highly esteemed by the Chinese, with a single character requiring as many as 33 strokes, and is written from top to bottom of the page and from left to right or, in many cases, from right to left.
The spoken language can be complicated by the fact that the dialects of the various provinces may differ as much from one another as two European languages. The Cantonese dialect spoken in Hong Kong (from the South China province of Kwangtung) is very difficult for foreigners to understand since it uses nine different musical tones to distinguish between the same syllables. Mandarin, the Chinese equivalent of the "Queen's English", is used only to a very limited extent. English is the normal means of communication with visitors and is widely understood by Hong Kong people, although their command of it may often be very limited.

Macau

The official language of Macau is Portuguese, but here too Cantonese Chinese is the tongue most commonly spoken, together with some Mandarin. Some people also speak French, Spanish and English, and in general visitors can get by using English.

English	Cantonese
bad	m ho
beer	beh jau
beautiful	ho leng
excuse me, I'm sorry	dui m jue
go	hoi
go away	tsau
good	ho
goodbye	joy geen
good morning	jo sun
hello (on telephone)	waai
help!	gau meng a
how are you?	nei ho ma?
fine, thank you	gay ho, nei yau sum
how much? (cost)	gay do tcheen a?
how many/much?	gay do a?
too expensive	tei gwai
I don't understand	ngoh m ming baak
left	jo
money	tcheen
Mr	sin saang
Mrs	taai taai
Miss	siu je
no	m hai
please	m goi
right	yau
tea (Chinese)	tcha
tea (English)	laai tcha
telephone	deen wah
thank you (for service or favor)	m goi

you are welcome, not at all	m sai m goi
thank you (for gift or hospitality)	doh je
not at all, don't mention it	m sai doh je
waiter, the bill, please	faw gay, my daan, m goi
Numbers:	
0	ling
1	yat
2	yee
3	saam
4	say
5	ng
6	lok
7	tchut
8	baat
9	gau
10	sup
Geographical terms:	
pass	au
island	chau
stream, valley	hang
village	heung
river	ho
market	hui
headland	kok
hill	ling
temple	miu
channel, passage	mun
south	nam
harbor, bay	o
rock, reef	pai
north	pak
west	sai
new	san
sand	sha
mountain	shan
rock, rocky hill	shek
beach	tarn
headland	tau
district	tei
village	tsuen
east	tung
clan village, home	uk
walled village	wai
beach	wan

Libraries

Hong Kong

The libraries likely to be of most interest to the ordinary visitor are the library in City Hall and the other public libraries run by the municipal authorities. The libraries of the Universities are more specialized. Most libraries have film, newspaper cutting and microfilm archives.
Enquiries should be addressed to the following numbers:

Alliance Française Library, 123 Hennessy Road, Hong Kong, tel. 5–277825

British Council Library, 255 Hennessy Road, Hong Kong, tel. 5–756501

City Hall Library, tel. 5–233688
See A to Z, City Hall
Open Mon.–Wed. and Fri. 9 a.m.–8 p.m., Sat. 9 a.m.–5 p.m., Sun. 9 a.m.–1 p.m.

Chinese University of Hong Kong Library, tel. 12–633111

Goethe-Institut Library, tel. 5–270088

University of Hong Kong Library, tel. 5–468161

Macau

Historical archive:
91–93 Ave. Conselheiro Ferreira do Almeida
Mon.–Sat. 9 a.m.–1 p.m. and 3–5 p.m.

National library:
89 Ave. Conselheiro Ferreira do Almeida
Mon.–Fri. 10 a.m.–10 p.m., Sat. 10 a.m.–8 p.m.

Lost property

Hong Kong has no lost property office, and objects found in streets and buildings are usually handed in at the nearest police station. The police regularly publish information in the newspapers about lost property in their possession. Enquiries: tel. 5–284284, ext. 236.

For items lost on public transport, apply to the appropriate lost property office:

China Motor Bus Co., tel. 5–616171
Kowloon Motor Bus Co., tel. 12–296161
Hong Kong Tramways, tel. 5–764321
Peak Tramway, tel. 5–220922
Mass Transit Railway, tel. 3–7585111
Kowloon–Canton Railway, tel. 3–646321

Markets

Hong Kong Island

The two most interesting markets on Hong Kong Island are the Poor Man's Night-club (see that entry in the A to Z section) and the Thieves' Market (see A to Z, Cat Street).
There is a large and interesting fish market in Aberdeen (see that entry in the A to Z section).
Food markets are to be found all over the city, as well as the occasional hawker. Itinerant dealers frequently congregate in particular streets.

Kowloon

There is a busy market in Reclamation Street, a turning off Battery Street on the right.
In the evening the market in Temple Street (to the right off Nathan Road) attracts large numbers of local people and visitors. See A to Z, Night Market.
There are also many food markets in Kowloon.

Shopping lanes

In many side streets, particularly on Hong Kong Island, are many little shops and booths where textiles (mostly local

Egg-seller in one of Hong Kong's markets

products) can be bought cheaply. Bargaining is in order in these local market lanes. Particularly worth visiting are Li Yuen Street East and Li Yuen Street West, which run between Queen's Road and Des Voeux Road. Other interesting little streets are Wing On Street and Pottinger Street.

Macau

Textiles and clothing at bargain prices can be found on a host of market stalls in the S. Domingos Market, Senate Square, and on the sidewalk stalls along Cinco de Outubro and Rua Palha. Stalls are also located in the Ave. da Infante D. Henrique and Ave. Almeida Ribeiro. Macau's flea market is in the alleys off the Rua das Estalagens, near St Paul's Church. See Shopping.

Motoring

With over 300,000 motor vehicles (1982), Hong Kong has almost perpetual traffic jams. The steadily increasing number of new registrations is causing the authorities great concern, for the city's streets are proving simply inadequate. There is practically no parking space in the central area, except in multi-story car parks. In 1982, measures were introduced to restrain the rate of growth in the numbers of private cars and motorcycles, e.g. higher tax on first registration, increase in license fees, more tax on gasoline. (Disabled drivers are exempt from these measures.)
The fines for illegal parking are high, and cars which are parked in the wrong place and interfere with the movement of traffic are towed away at once. Visitors to Hong Kong, unless they are familiar with the road system and with traffic conditions in the

city, will be well advised to avoid adding to the general traffic chaos by driving themselves.

Vehicles travel on the left, with overtaking on the right. Unless otherwise indicated by traffic signs, vehicles coming from the right have priority – though this does not apply to traffic coming out of a side road into a main road. There are few roundabouts, but here, too, traffic coming from the right has priority. Other motoring regulations are much the same as in Europe or North America.

The Government Information Service publishes a small booklet on the Highway Code, which is worth studying before driving in Hong Kong. Visitors must have an international driving license.

Speed limit

The speed limit is 30 m.p.h. in built-up areas, and 60 m.p.h. elsewhere.

Breakdown assistance

If you have a breakdown in a hired car the hire firm should be informed.

For a breakdown outside normal working hours the Hong Kong Automobile Association (HKAA, tel. 5–737474) should be contacted. Car hire firms often have an agreement with the HKAA for providing out-of-hours breakdown assistance.

In case of breakdown in a vehicle other than a hired car assistance should be sought either from the HKAA or from a garage dealing in the particular make.

Macau

Private cars cannot be taken into Macau where the only vehicles available for hire are jeep-style mini-mokes.

See Car hire and Parking garages.

Movie theaters

The Chinese are addicted moviegoers, and the movie theaters of Hong Kong offer a wide range of attractions, from local productions (mostly kung fu films) to the latest American box office successes. Sex films are adapted to local moral standards by the censorship, but pornographic films are made available by private entrepreneurs.

The following is a very brief selection of movie theaters.

Hong Kong

Cathy, 125 Wanchai Road, tel. 5–724745
Hoover, 64 Yee Wo Street, tel. 5–762371
King's, 34 Queen's Road Central, tel. 5–225313
Lee, 27 Percival Street, tel. 5–776319
Palace, 280 Gloucester Road, tel. 5–795179
Pearl, Paterson Street, tel. 5–776351
Queen's, 37 Queen's Road Central, tel. 5–766241

Kowloon

Empress, Sai Yeung Choi Street, tel. 3–809570
London, 219 Nathan Road, tel. 3–661056
Majestic, 334 Nathan Road, tel. 3–847115
Ocean, Harbour Centre, tel. 3–678091
Washington, 92 Parkes Street, tel. 3–310405

Museums

Hong Kong

Art Gallery of Institute of Chinese Studies
See A to Z

Flagstaff House Museum of Tea
See A to Z

Fung Ping Shan Museum
See A to Z

Hong Kong Museum of Art
See A to Z

Hong Kong Museum of Chinese Historical Relics
See A to Z

Hong Kong Museum of History
See A to Z

Space Museum
See A to Z

Macau

Museu Luís de Camões
See A to Z

Residência do Dr Sun Yat-sen
See A to Z

Admission charges

In general there are no admission charges for the museums listed.

Nightlife

Hong Kong

Hong Kong's nightlife is much more varied than it used to be, although the colony is still particularly famed for its bars. The bigger hotels put on dinner shows, some of them with really big names which are advertised in the daily press. The host of Chinese night-clubs such as Metropole, North Point, etc. have regular bands, most of them Philippino groups.

Popular discos include Disco Disco (40 D'Anguilar Street, Central), Hollywood Boulevard (Elizabeth House, Causeway Bay) and Casablanca (in Aberdeen).

The Lan Kwai Fong quarter in Central District (lower end of D'Anguilar Street, a block above Queen's Road) has become very lively of late. Besides Disco Disco already referred to it also contains the adjoining Underground Club, as well as the California Bar and Grill, an up-market cocktail lounge, with American West Coast cooking and dancing till 4 a.m. 1997, a restaurant with a dance club and coffee shop, is in the alley behind it.

In Kowloon the New World Centre in Tsimshatsui's Salisbury Road has become a popular night-time haunt, with its unusual City Bar and a whole group of other bars such as Country and Western, plus the Cabaret Night-club, a hostess club that welcomes couples as well as singles.

The pubs include the Godown in the basement of Sutherland House, Central, which is also known for its food, the Dickens

Bar in the Excelsior Hotel, Causeway Bay which has jazz on Sunday afternoons, and the Blacksmith's Arms, 16 Minden Avenue, Tsimshatsui, which is good for a pint of beer at the bar. Hong Kong's famous bars are quite entertaining on a first visit, and the best ones, almost all of which have Japanese names and have been adapted to the tastes of that country's businessmen, can now almost be termed classic. Most of them are quite simple bars, as can be found in most Asian cities. The only difference is that they are markedly more expensive and frequently topless. There are still quite a few of the old girlie bars, and there are also various agencies operating "escort services".

With the departure of American troops from the war in South-East Asia the bar district has lost much of its color, and two new trends have been emerging. One is the advent of more "gentlemen's clubs", mostly geared to expense account businessmen.

These vie with the Japanese version, and are very spacious by Hong Kong standards, with big dancefloors, at least two (usually Philippino) bands, singers and up to a thousand hostesses. These establishments are very expensive but also full up throughout the week. The best known are the New Tonnochy Night-club, the Club Celebrity and the Dai-Ichi in Wan Chai, while in Tsimshatsui there are the Club Deluxe, the Club New World and the China City.

The second trend is towards cheaper disco pubs designed for young people with less to spend, often not requiring a cover charge. These are mainly frequented by Philippino girls and soldiers or sailors on furlough. The current favorites are Makati Inn, 5th Avenue, Crossroad and The In Place.

Hong Kong's dance-halls are virtually exclusively Chinese, but Europeans can find them an interesting experience as well. There is no alcohol, the only drink is tea and most of the girls (hardly any of whom speak English) are there as dancing partners only. The Oriental, Jordan Road, Kowloon, is very popular.

Macau

Nightlife in Macau centers on its four casinos that are chiefly patronized by Chinese gamblers from nearby Hong Kong.

The Casino de Lisboa (see entry in Macau A to Z), in the hotel of the same name, has both Western and Chinese games, ranging from roulette, boule, craps, blackjack, one-armed bandits (here called "hungry tiger") and fruit machines, to fan tan, sik po, pai kau, etc. The Macau Palace, moored in the inner harbor and looking like a Mississippi steamboat, contains a casino, restaurant, bar and night-club. Both these casinos are open 24 hours a day. Gambling is also to be found in the Jai Alai Palace, where there is also betting on the results of its version of "pelota", and in the Kam Pek casino in the center of town, which has Chinese forms of gambling only.

There are two performances nightly of the Crazy Paris Revue, complete with European-style showgirls, in the Dom Pedro V Theatre's Mona Lisa Hall, and the Portas do Sol restaurant in the Hotel Lisboa puts on Portuguese folk-dancing at 10 p.m. on uneven dates of the month. Discos have also been opened in the new Macau hotels, such as the Green Parrot in the Hyatt Regency Hotel, the Skylight disco in Hotel Presidente, which also has the Royal Disco, the Ritz Night Club in the Jai Alai Palace and the Mikado Big I Disco in the new wing of the Hotel Lisboa.

Opening times

Hong Kong
Shops and offices

Central area, Hong Kong Island: Mon.–Sat. 9 a.m.–6 p.m. Queen's Road and Des Voeux Road: sometimes from 10 a.m., in the evening until 8 p.m.
Business center, Kowloon, and Causeway Bay, Hong Kong: 10 a.m.–10 p.m.; frequently also on Sundays.

Public offices

From 9 or 9.30 a.m. to 4 or 5 p.m.; on Saturdays from 9 or 9.30 a.m. to noon or 1 p.m.

Diplomatic missions

Weekdays 9 a.m.–noon; sometimes also in the afternoon.

Banks

See under Banks.

Business calls

These are normally paid between 10 a.m. and 12.30 p.m. and between 2.30 and 5 p.m.

Private calls

The usual time to call on friends or acquaintances is about 8 or 8.30 in the evening. It is normal to give prior notice of a call.

Macau

Shops in Macau have no fixed opening times, but as a general rule they are open from about 8 or 9 in the morning until at least 7 in the evening, and often much later. Small shops tend largely to close in the lunch-hour.

Parking

Hong Kong has 48 multi-story parking lots, eight of them run by the local authorities, but as the number of cars on the road keeps increasing they tend to soon get full up. There is parking at all the big hotels, public buildings (e.g. City Hall), the New World Centre, Ocean Terminal, Ocean Centre, the ferry terminals, Windsor House, Murray Parkhouse, etc.

Photography

Film is expensive so you should be sure to take all that you want with you. Modern film is proof against tropical conditions but it is wise to protect it against excessive temperature changes by keeping it in the special containers provided by many manufacturers. However, these do not provide full protection against the X-rays used for airport baggage controls, so it is a good idea to keep your films, whether exposed or not, in your hand baggage.
It is not advisable to have your film developed abroad since you cannot be sure of the result, so if you do not want to carry your exposed films with you it is wise to send it back home by registered mail where it can be developed professionally.
However photogenic or picturesque the appearance, clothing and behavior of the local people may appear, they should not be photographed unless permission has been obtained beforehand. This is particularly true where religious practices are involved, as well as anything that might be of a military nature such as bridges, airfields, etc. Much of what looks picturesque to us is seen as simply backward by the locals, and they object to slums being considered quaint backgrounds for people's holiday snaps.

Postal service

General Post Office

The General Post Office is close to the Star Ferry Pier on Hong Kong Island. There is a post office opposite the Ocean Centre in central Kowloon.

Postal rates

Hong Kong
First-class airmail letter rates for countries in Zone 1 (Asian countries from Japan to Pakistan) are currently HK$1 for the first 10 grams and $0·60 for each additional 10 grams, and for Zone 2 countries (Europe, America, Australia, etc.) are HK$1·30 and $0·70.
Aerograms can be obtained from any post office and can be sent anywhere at a uniform rate of HK$1.
The postal services are speedy and reliable, with airmail to Europe and Australia taking 4–5 days, to North America 6–8 days.
For further information on postal or parcel services ask at any post office or call the Post Office Enquiry Bureau on 5–2671222.

Macau
Similar postal rates apply in Macau, but it is a good idea to get your hotel reception desk to look after your mail for you since you will have a long wait in the post office.
See Telegrams and Telephone services.

Public holidays and Festivals

The date of most of the Chinese public holidays varies each year on the Western calendar because they are fixed according to the thirteen lunar months a year, although public holidays commemorating historical events tend to have fixed dates.

Hong Kong

1 January — New Year's Day

January–February

Chinese New Year. This is the first day of the first lunar month in a new year, which falls between 21 January and 18 February in the Western calendar. This is the most important festival in the Chinese calendar and continues for three days of parties and everyone wishing everyone else good luck and good fortune.
Lantern Festival. 14 days after the Chinese New Year's Day, when lanterns are hung up everywhere.

February

Hong Kong Arts Festival. First three weeks of February, with international artists in plays, concerts, exhibitions, etc. Advance reservation is recommended.

March–April

Ching Ming Festival. 8th day of the 3rd lunar month, a day for commemorating the dead with visits to family graves and traditional rites.
Good Friday, Easter Monday.

Birthday of Tin Hau, patron saint of seafarers to whom many local temples are dedicated and particularly beloved by the Hong Kong boat people. Much of the festivities is centered on the Tai Miu Temple at Joss House Bay when there are lion dances and processions of gaily decorated boats carrying gift-laden altars. — April–May

Cheung Chau Bun Festival. A week-long Buddhist festival on the island of Cheung Chau, when the locals are not supposed to eat any meat, climaxing in a colorful procession and a ceremony of scrambling for lucky buns. These used to be piled up in very tall towers but these have been reduced in size and climbing them has been forbidden since a couple collapsed several years ago.
Lord Buddha's birthday in May is particularly celebrated at the Po Lin Monastery on Lantau Island. — May

Tuen Ng, the Dragon Boat Festival, the most famous and endearing of the Crown Colony's annual events. It is held in early June to coincide with the time when the poet and statesman Chu Yuan is supposed to have drowned himself in 332 B.C. in despair at the corruption of his time. According to legend the boats are those of the fishermen who rowed to save him. The festival's main race takes place in Tai Po and there are others at Aberdeen, Stanley, Tuen Mun, Shu Tin and Cheung Chau. The dragon boats are long and narrow, with a dragon's head on the bow, propelled by 50 oarsmen to the beat of a drum amidships. — June

The Queen's Birthday. — 16 June

Hungry Ghost Festival – Yue Lan. Burning special paper money and making offerings of food, etc. are said to ease the hunger of the ghosts of those who have died without a family or a grave and are condemned to wander homeless. — July–August

Liberation Day, last Monday in August. Commemoration of Hong Kong's liberation from the Japanese in 1945. — August

Mid-Autumn Festival. One of the most important of the annual festivals, when traditional moon cakes are eaten and children carry lanterns shaped like fishes and birds as the people of Hong Kong go for night-time picnics in all the open spaces to gaze at the moon which is supposed to be at its most beautiful at this time.
Birthday of Confucius, celebrated in the Confucian temple in Causeway Bay. This coincides with the Asian Arts Festival. — September–October

Chung Yeung. People go for picnics at high points in the colony, a tradition dating back to the Han dynasty when a family were rightly advised that by doing so they would avoid disaster. — October

Christmas Day and Boxing Day. — 25 and 26 December

Macau
New Year's Day. — 1 January

Chinese New Year. Lantern Festival (see Hong Kong, above). — January–February

March	The Procession of Our Lord of Passos. A festival unique to Macau when on the first weekend of Lent the statue of Jesus from St Augustine's is carried in procession across the town.
March–April	Festival of the God Tutei. Good Friday, Easter Monday.
April	Ching Ming Festival (see Hong Kong, above). A Ma Festival (cf. Birthday of Tin Hau, Hong Kong), Macau's most important Chinese festival, which takes place on the 23rd day of the 3rd moon.
25 April	Anniversary of the Revolution in Portugal.
1 May	Labout Day.
May	Procession of Our Lady of Fatima. Festival of Tam Kong (a week-long celebration on the island of Coloane). Bathing of the Buddha, when Buddhist shrines are washed and purified.
May–June	Corpus Christi. Camoes and Portuguese Communities Day.
June	Dragon Boat Festival (see Hong Kong, above).
24 June	Feast of St John the Baptist (patron saint of Macau).
13 July	Feast of the Battle of 13 July, on Taipa and Coloane islands only, commemorating a Macanese victory over pirates in 1910.
15 August	Feast of the Assumption of Our Lady.
September–October	Mid-Autumn or Mooncake Festival (see Hong Kong, above). Hungry Ghost Festival, Confucius' Birthday (see Hong Kong, above).
1 October	National Day of the People's Republic of China (unofficial public holiday).
5 October	Republic Day, marking the birth of the Portuguese Republic in 1910. Cheung Yeung, the 9th day of the 9th moon when Chinese families visit graves and give offerings.
1 and 2 November	All Saints and All Souls days.
1 December	Independence Day, commemorating Portugal's independence from Spain in 1640.
8 December	Feast of the Immaculate Conception.
22 December	Winter Solstice.
24 and 25 December	Christmas Eve, Christmas Day.

See Events, Folk traditions.

Public transport

Hong Kong

Mass Transit Railway (MTR)

Opened in 1980, this air-conditioned subway system runs for about $15\frac{1}{2}$ miles/26 km from Hong Kong Island to Tsuen Wan new town in the west on one route and east to Kwun Tong on the other. It carries more than 1·2 million people a year and runs from 6 in the morning to 1 a.m. at night. Tickets can be bought with various coins from automatic ticket machines.

Trams

Quaint old double-decker trams run from Kennedy Town, West Point, on Hong Kong Island, through Central District to Causeway Bay, North Point and Shau Kei Wan in the east, with a branch line running inland to Happy Valley. From the top deck you get a good view of the hustle and bustle of Hong Kong life swirling all around you.

Victoria Peak Tram

This funicular operates from 7 a.m. to midnight daily and the 8-minute trip from Garden Road to the top of Victoria Peak overlooking Hong Kong from the south is a most impressive experience (see Hong Kong A to Z).

Bus services

Buses run from Kai Tak Airport to Hong Kong Island every 20 minutes. Most of the big hotels have their own shuttle services, with their drivers, in uniform, waiting just outside Customs.
Hong Kong itself has a dense network of bus services to all parts of the Crown Colony. The buses, which run from 6 a.m. till midnight, get very crowded in the rush-hour but are otherwise a pleasant way to get about. Information on timetables, etc., is obtainable from the Hong Kong Tourist Association. The drivers don't speak much English and you pay on entry, so keep some small change handy.

Minibuses, maxicabs

Many routes in the Crown Colony are served by public minibuses. These are yellow with red stripes and are a speedy and comfortable alternative form of transport to taxis. Minibus stops for routes serving Wan Chai, Causeway Bay and all destinations in the east sector are on the west side of the Connaught Building, Star Ferry Pier. The green-striped maxicabs run from the east side of City Hall to Victoria Peak.

Taxis

The easiest way of getting about in Hong Kong is to take a taxi. All taxis are fitted with meters; but it is as well to check that the driver switches on the meter only when you get in, since otherwise there is a risk that you may be paying the previous passenger's fare a well. Drivers usually have a reasonable knowledge of English. If you are going to some out-of-the-way part of the city, however, it is a good idea to give the driver a slip of paper with your destination written in Chinese characters (ask a member of the hotel staff to write it for you).
At rush hours and weekends it is difficult to get a taxi, in spite of the fact that there are over 8000 in Hong Kong and Kowloon and 750 in the New Territories. For journeys between Hong Kong Island and Kowloon through the Cross-Harbour Tunnel, toll charges are payable in addition to the fare shown on the meter; tolls must be paid for the return journey, since taxis operate either only on Hong Kong Island or only in Kowloon. There is an extra charge for large pieces of luggage.

NO RIGHT TURN
不准右轉
AJI-NO
味の
世界馳名
角
KEEP
LEFT
77

There are taxi ranks at the Star Ferry Pier on both sides of the harbor. Taxis can also be hailed in the street – though the driver will sometimes ignore your signal if the traffic situation is difficult or you are awkwardly placed.

Rickshaws

There are still some rickshaws in the center of Hong Kong and Kowloon but they are only a tourist gimmick now and the rickshaw men will charge to have their photo taken as well as for providing a ride. Make sure you fix the price before you take a photo – and that it is agreed in Hong Kong, not American, dollars (about HK$10–20 is the going rate for a posed snap, while the charge for a five-minute ride is supposed to be about HK$20).

Car rental

Hong Kong has car rental firms but the traffic is so heavy in the central districts that other ways of getting about would be more sensible. If you want to explore the New Territories or the south side of Hong Kong Island it's a good idea to share a vehicle with several people. See Car rental.

Ferries

See entry.

Rail

See Rail travel, Railroad stations.

Macau

Taxis

Since the drivers of Macau's taxis (which are black with a beige roof) speak little English it is a good idea to take with you the map of Macau provided by the Tourist Office so that you can point out the name of your destination. Make sure the meter is set at the ordinary fare if you are making a short journey. For longer trips you can negotiate a special deal but make sure that the driver is left in no doubt of what has been agreed – the price in patacas, the inclusion of all the passengers, etc. – before you set out. Journeys to Taipa and Coloane, which require crossing by bridge or causeway, put about 5 patacas more on top of the meter.

Car rental

The only vehicles currently for rental in Macau are mini-mokes, nippy little open jeeps. Drivers need an international driving license. See Car rental.

Bus services

Buses run in the city, between the harbour and city center and out to the islands, from 7 a.m. to midnight. Open-topped double-decker buses also run in the summer. The most convenient stop is in front of the Hotel Lisboa.

Pedicabs

These tricycle-drawn two-seater cabs are a pleasant way to go sightseeing in the city, although they are not able to climb hills so they are not suitable for touring further afield. The drivers tend to speak some English and know what visitors like to see, but fares should be negotiated because they will usually ask twice as much as they'll settle for.

Bicycles

Bicycles can be rented for about 5 patacas an hour from various hotels, shops on Ave. Dom Joao IV and from a shop next to the Taipa bus terminal. They may not be ridden across the bridge from Macau to Taipa.

◀ *Riding the green train to North Point*

Macau Tourism Department, "Guide to Macau".

Montalto de Jesus, C. A., "Historic Macao" (Reprint), Oxford University Press, from Department of Tourism, Macao.

"Travel Trade Handbook", Department of Tourism, Macao.

Rather similar to Shann Davis's "Viva Macau" which combines contemporary photos with historical background, there is also Harry Rolnick's "A Glimpse of Glory", which is in English, Portuguese and Chinese. Austin Coates's "City of Broken Promises" tells the true story of Chinese businesswoman Marta Merop, while Robert Elegant's "Manchu" has descriptions of Macau in the last days of the Imperial dynasties.
"Macau Travel Talk", an occasional magazine, can be obtained from Portuguese Tourist Offices abroad while, in Hong Kong, maps, guides such as the Guide to Macau, etc. can be had from the Macau Tourist Information Bureau, Room 1729, Star House, Kowloon, or from the Macau Department of Tourism, which also publishes free leaflets on hotels, restaurants, sightseeing, etc. These too can be obtained from most of the big hotels.

Restaurants

Hong Kong
The following list is merely a brief selection from the immense number of restaurants in Hong Kong. Advance booking is recommended because they are always crowded at midday and between 7 and 9.30 in the evening. It is best to book your table from your hotel because little English is spoken in most restaurants, although menus in English are always available.
Little English is spoken either in the many little eating-houses serving chicken, duck, pork and other tempting dishes, but here you can order what you want simply by pointing to it. Anyone on a tight budget should go for rice or noodle dishes, while the many takeaway food stalls where, for instance, you can get won ton, the thick noodle soup, are even cheaper.

Hot-pot

One of the cheapest gastronomic delights is "hot-pot", which is best eaten in the picturesque setting of the Poor Man's Night-club (see Hong Kong A to Z), where you can prepare this fondu-style dish yourself.

Aberdeen

Aberdeen's famous floating restaurants come at the other end of the price range, but the incomparable atmosphere of this floating city of junks, the oldest part of Hong Kong, makes them well worth a visit. A meal there, including the trip out by sampan, works out at about £10.
For a description of the various regional cuisines see Food and drink.

Chiu Chow cuisine

Hong Kong Island
Chiuchow Garden Restaurant
Hennessy Centre (2nd and 3rd floors)
500 Hennessy Road, Causeway Bay, Hong Kong
tel. 5–773391
Connaught Centre (basement), Central, Hong Kong
tel. 5–258246

Pak Shings
23 Hysan Avenue, Hong Kong
tel. 5–768886

Kowloon
Chiuchow Garden Restaurant
Tsim Sha Tsui Centre (2nd floor), East Tsimshatsui, Kowloon
tel. 3–688772

City Chiuchow Restaurant
East Ocean Centre (1st floor)
98 Granville Road, East Tsimshatsui, Kowloon
tel. 3–7245383, 3–7236226

Golden Island Bird's Nest (Chiu Chau) Restaurant Ltd.
25 Carnarvon Road (3rd and 4th floors), Tsimshatsui, Kowloon
tel. 3–695211

New Golden Red (Chiu Chau) Restaurant Ltd.
13–15 Prat Avenue, Tsimshatsui, Kowloon
tel. 3–666822

Tsui Hung
15 Saigon Street, Kowloon
tel. 3–385947

Hakka cuisine

Kowloon
The Home Restaurant Ltd.
19–20 Hanoi Road, Tsimshatsui, Kowloon
tel. 3–665876

Cantonese cuisine

Hong Kong Island
Blue Ocean Restaurant
Aberdeen Marina Tower (9th floor)
8 Shum Wan Road, Wong Chuk Hang, Hong Kong
tel. 5–559415–8

Boil & Boil Wonderful Restaurant
Food Street, Causeway Bay, Hong Kong
tel. 5–779788

Diamond Restaurant Ltd.
265–275 Des Voeux Road Central, Hong Kong
tel. 5–444921
483 Lockhart Road, Causeway Bay, Hong Kong
tel. 5–8912575

Flower Lounge Restaurant Ltd.
Shop B (ground floor), Lockhart House
441 Lockhart Road, Causeway Bay, Hong Kong
tel. 5–8937977

Fook Lam Moon Restaurant Ltd.
459 Lockhart Road (ground floor), Causeway Bay, Hong Kong
tel. 5–8912639

Jade Garden Restaurant
Hyde Park Mansion
53 Paterson Street, Causeway Bay, Hong Kong
tel. 5–778282

Swire House (1st floor), Central, Hong Kong
tel. 5–239966
1 Hysan Avenue, Wanchai, Hong Kong
tel. 5–779332
Entertainment Building (basement)
30–34 Queen's Road Central, Hong Kong
tel. 5–234071

Jumbo Floating Restaurant
Shum Wan, Wong Chuk Hang, Hong Kong
tel. 5–539111

King Bun Restaurant Ltd.
158 Queen's Road Central, Hong Kong
tel. 5–446743

Luk Yu Tea House and Restaurant Ltd.
26 Stanley Street, Central, Hong Kong
tel. 5–235464

Maxim's Palace Chinese Restaurant
World Trade Centre (1st floor), Causeway Bay, Hong Kong
tel. 5–760288

North Park Restaurant Ltd.
440 Jaffe Road, Causeway Bay, Hong Kong
tel. 5–8912940

North Sea Fishing Village Co. Ltd.
455 King's Road, North Point, Hong Kong
tel. 5–630187

Pearl City Restaurant Ltd.
Pearl City Mansion
36 Paterson Street, Causeway Bay, Hong Kong
tel. 5–778226

Pimelea Restaurant Ltd.
Far East Finance Centre (basement)
16 Harcourt Road, Central, Hong Kong
tel. 5–202212

Ping Shan Restaurant Ltd.
Lido Complex, 28 Beach Road, Repulse Bay, Hong Kong
tel. 5–921557

Riverside Restaurant
Food Street, Causeway Bay, Hong Kong
tel. 5–779733

Sea Palace Floating Restaurant
Shum Wan, Wong Chuk Hang, Hong Kong
tel. 5–527340

Sun Tung Lok Shark's Fin Restaurant
78 Morrison Hill Road, Causeway Bay, Hong Kong
tel. 5–748261

Tai Pak Seafood Restaurant Ltd.
Shum Wan, Wong Chuk Hang, Hong Kong
tel. 5–525953

Tao Yuan Restaurant
Great Eagle Centre (3rd floor)
23 Harbour Road, Wan Chai, Hong Kong
tel. 5–738080

Tsui Hang Village Restaurant
New World Tower (2nd floor)
16–18 Queen's Road Central, Hong Kong
tel. 5–242012

United Restaurant
United Centre (5th and 6th floors)
95 Queensway, Central, Hong Kong
tel. 5–295010

*Vegi Food Kitchen
Flat B, Highland Mansion (ground floor)
8 Cleveland Street, Causeway Bay, Hong Kong
tel. 5–7906660

Water World Restaurant
Ocean Park, Wong Chuk Hang Road, Aberdeen, Hong Kong
tel. 5–558373

*Wishful Cottage Vegetarian Restaurant
336 Lockhart Road (ground floor), Causeway Bay, Hong Kong
tel. 5–734194

Yung Kee Restaurant
36–40 Wellington Street, Central, Hong Kong
tel. 5–232343

Kowloon
Can Do Restaurant
37 Cameron Road, Tsimshatsui, Kowloon
tel. 3–7218183

Capital Restaurant and Night Club
36–44 Nathan Road, Tsimshatsui, Kowloon
tel. 3–681844

*Choi Kun Heung Vegetarian Restaurant
219E Nathan Road (ground floor), Yaumati, Kowloon
tel. 3–667185

Chui Heung Lau Restaurant Ltd.
Peninsula Centre (basement), East Tsimshatsui, Kowloon
tel. 3–663966

Diamond Restaurant Ltd.
26 Sai Yeung Choi Street, Mongkok, Kowloon
tel. 3–854030

Flower Lounge Restaurant (Kowloon) Ltd.
3 Peace Avenue (ground and 1st floor), Homatin, Kowloon
tel. 3–7156557

Fook Lam Moon (Kowloon) Restaurant Ltd.
31 Mody Road (ground floor), East Tsimshatsui, Kowloon
tel. 3–687688

Peking Garden Restaurant
Star House (3rd floor), Salisbury Road, Tsimshatsui, Kowloon
tel. 3–698211
Empire Centre (1st floor), East Tsimshatsui, Kowloon
tel. 3–687879

Peking Restaurant
227 Nathan Road, Yaumati, Kowloon
tel. 3–671315

Pleasure Restaurant and Night Club Ltd.
45–47 Carnarvon Road, Tsimshatsui, Kowloon
tel. 3–660408

Shing Tao Restaurant Ltd.
6–8 Jordan Road (1st and 2nd floors), Yaumati, Kowloon
tel. 3–7243832

Spring Deer Restaurant Ltd.
42 Mody Road, East Tsimshatsui, Kowloon
tel. 3–664012

Sun Hung Cheung Hing Restaurant Ltd.
35A Kimberley Road, Tsimshatsui, Kowloon
tel. 3–693435

Tien Heung Lau Restaurant
18C Austin Avenue, Tsimshatsui, Kowloon
tel. 3–689660

Shanghai cuisine

Hong Kong Island
Shanghai Garden Restaurant
Shop G30 and 33, 115–124 and 126 Hutchinson House, 10 Harcourt Road, Central, Hong Kong
tel. 5–238322, 5–248181
Hennessy Centre (1st floor)
500 Hennessy Road, Causeway Bay, Hong Kong
tel. 5–779996, 5–7950395

Kowloon
Great Shanghai Restaurant Ltd.
26 Prat Avenue, Tsimshatsui, Kowloon
tel. 3–668158

Wu Kong Shanghai Restaurant
Alpha House (basement)
27 Nathan Road, Tsimshatsui, Kowloon
tel. 3–667244

Szechuan cuisine

Hong Kong Island
Cleveland Szechuan Restaurant
6 Cleveland Street, Causeway Bay, Hong Kong
tel. 5–765617

Pep'N Chilli
Shop F (ground floor)
12–22 Blue Pool Road, Happy Valley, Hong Kong
tel. 5–738251

Red Pepper Restaurant
7 Lan Fong Road, Causeway Bay, Hong Kong
tel. 5–768046

Szechuen Lau Restaurant
466 Lockhart Road (ground floor), Causeway Bay, Hong Kong
tel. 5–8919027

Sichuan Garden Restaurant
Gloucester Tower (3rd floor), Central, Hong Kong
tel. 5–214433

Kowloon
Greenvilla Restaurant
27A Granville Road (ground floor), Tsimshatsui, Kowloon
tel. 3–7213238

Lotus Pond Sechuen Restaurant
Phase IV (ground floor)
15 Harbour City, Tsimshatsui, Kowloon
tel. 3–7241088

Western cuisine

Hong Kong's Western cuisine has improved considerably in recent times, and reaches a truly international level in the top hotels, especially in East Tsimshatsui. The Regent House has two excellent restaurants, the Steak House (American steaks and salad) and the Plum (nouvelle cuisine). The Royal Garden's Lalique Restaurant has a pleasant atmosphere and offers such recherché dishes as snipe, smoked salmon, fresh lobster, pheasant, etc. Also highly rated are Gaddi's and Chesa, Swiss restaurants in the Peninsula Hotel, Kowloon, the Margaux, in the Shangri La Hotel, the Mandarin Grill and Pierrot, both in the Mandarin Hotel, the Chinnery Bar and various restaurants in the Hilton Hotel.
Two other hotels where you can dine out in the evening opened recently in Tsimshatsui are the Marco Polo, with its very Gallic La Brasserie, the Coffee Mill, which has more of a South American flavor, and the Festival coffee-shop, its theme being Scotland's Edinburgh Festival. The Prince Hotel, in the same building on Canton Road, has a grill, the Rib Room, a Spanish-style coffee-shop and an English pub, the Tavern, which also serves snacks.
Au Trou Normand, 6 Carnarvon Road, Kowloon, has good French cuisine. Jimmy's Kitchen (Ashley Road, Kowloon Centre, 1st floor) and Palm Restaurant (38 Lock Road, basement) both serve excellent steaks. Jimmy's (1 Wyndham Street) and Landau's (257 Gloucester Road, near the Embassy) are both on Hong Kong Island. Other specialty restaurants are the Sheikh (Arabic), the Beverley Hills Delicatessen, and Italian restaurants such as La Taverna, Rigoletto, Spaghetti House and the more expensive Café d'Amigo at 79A Wongneichong Road, opposite the Happy Valley racetrack.

Fast food

Hong Kong has countless fast food outlets, not least being those on "Food Street", two blocks east of the Excelsior Hotel, where there are two dozen restaurants of all kinds. Tex-Mex food can be obtained in the Casa Mexicana, and in Lindy's, both in the Lindy Centre, Causeway Bay. The Bull and Bear (Hutchinson House, Charter Road, Central District) has an

English pub atmosphere and, like the Jockey (Swire House, Charter Road, Central District), serves steaks, chicken, sausages, eggs and bacon, etc.

Non-Chinese Asian cuisine

Hong Kong also has several good restaurants serving non-Chinese cuisine from other parts of Asia. These include:
Japanese: The Yamato, 74 Queen's Road, Central District.
Indian: The Maharajah, 222 Wan Cahir Road, Wan Chai.
Korean: The Manna Korean Restaurant, near Hyatt Hotel, Nathan Road, Kowloon.
The Koreana, Pearson Street, Causeway Bay.
Indonesian: The Indonesian 26 Leighton Road, near Green Gardens Hotel.
Thai: King's Hotel Coffee Shop, 473 Nathan Road, Yaumati, Kowloon (only until 7.30 p.m.).
Vietnamese: Arc en Ciel, 57B Paterson Street, Causeway Bay.
Perfume River, 51–53 Hennessy Road, corner of Percival Street.
Yin Ping, 24 Cannon Street, Causeway Bay.

Macau
Restaurants offering anything other than Chinese or European cuisine tend not to last long in Macau, although Thai restaurants are something of an exception. A service charge of 10 per cent and tax of 5 per cent is added to all restaurant bills. There are good restaurants in the big hotels and the following list is a selection of eating-places outside the hotels.

Chinese cuisine

Macau
Asian
Jai Alai Palace (1st floor)
tel. 87109

Fok Lam Mun
Ave. da Amizade
tel. 86883

Fu Wa
11–13 Rua Dr Pedro Jose Lobo
tel. 76456

Jade
30 Ave. Almeirio Ribeiro
tel. 75126

Yat Yuen (Canidrome)
Ave. do Gen. Castelo Branco
tel. 574417

Long Kei
7 Largo do Senado
tel. 573970
(Specialty: bird's nest soup)

Ocean
Ave. da Amizade
tel. 71533

New Palace
(Floating Restaurant)
Inner Harbour
tel. 574480

Pun Quay
44 Rua da Praia Grande
tel. 75934

Tai Sam Un
41 Rua da Caldeira
tel. 76596

Tsui Hang Chun
11B Rua da Praia Grande
tel. 81618

Taipa
Fu Lai
Macao Trotting Club, Taipa
tel. 88501

Local Macau cuisine

Riquexó
69 Ave. Sidoñio Pais
tel. 76204

A Cozinha
57 Ave. da Amizade
Edificio Kam Va Kok, 1. andar
tel. 552502

Portuguese cuisine

Macau
Henri's
4G–H Ave. da Republica
tel. 76207
(Specialty: "African Chicken")

Fat Siu Lau
64 Rua da Felicidade
tel. 573585
(Specialty: roast pigeon)

Português
16 Rua do Campo
tel. 75445

Panda
4–8 Rue Carlos Eugénio (ground floor)
tel. 27338

Solmar
11 Rua da Praia Grande
tel. 574391

Coloane
Saludes
13 B. Ripa, Coloane
tel. 28228
(Specialties: crab, cod, sardines, rabbit)

Saludes II, an offshoot of the original restaurant, has been opened at Hac Sa Beach

Taipa
Pinocchio
4 Rua do Sol, Taipa
tel. 27128
(Specialties: roast quail, crab in chili sauce)

Other Western cuisine

Algarve Sol
41–43 Rua Comandante Mata e Oliveira
tel. 89007

Imperador
8–10 Rua Comandante Mata e Oliveira
tel. 75654

Jai Alai
Jai Alai Palace
tel. 81866

Kai Kai
54 Ave. Infante D. Henrique
tel. 574202

Shangri La
13A Ave. Horta e Costa
tel. 89199

Roma
34A Rua Nova à Guia
tel. 81799

Shopping

Hong Kong

Hong Kong certainly deserves its reputation as Asia's shopper's paradise, although that doesn't mean to say that prices there are necessarily much lower than elsewhere. The attractions of its free market, attracting tourists from all over the world, also ensure that vast amounts are there to be spent on all that the Far East has to offer, whatever the quality, and so prices can be higher than they ought to be. This is because bargaining is taken for granted, even in the most reputable shops. There are no precise rules but as a general rule you should get the price reduced by 10 to 20 per cent, often even more. It's best to start off by offering half the asking-price, then take it slowly from there. Only department stores and the 70 plus Red China stores operate fixed prices.
Few reputable shops sell fakes such as Swiss watches with a genuine outer case but works made in Hong Kong, but you should only buy clocks, cameras, etc. in specialty shops which are accredited dealers, and you should insist on also having the manufacturer's guarantee – not the dealer's, which will be worthless when you get back home.
Bargaining is also in order in the shops that are members of the Hong Kong Tourist Association, recognized by their red junk logo. The HKTA also publishes a list of reputable shops with agents' recommended retail prices in its "Official Guide to Shopping, Eating Out and Services", available free of charge from their information centers. Favorite items with tourists are table linen, embroidery, silk, brocade, pewter, copper, jewelry,

jade, ivory, carpets, bamboo furniture, china, ceramics, Asian objets d'art, watches, cameras and electrical goods.
Hong Kong's tailors are famous for their skill and speed and in extreme instances you can get a suit made to measure in 48 hours, although you get a much better result if you can wait a week for it. The prices are no longer as reasonable as they used to be some years ago. For women's clothes a made to measure outfit can take several weeks in the better dressmaker's shops, so it's better to buy off the peg. Furs are relatively cheap. Shoes can be made to measure, although there may be problems with the larger sizes.
The major shopping area for tourists extends on both sides of the Star Ferry Pier for Hong Kong and Kowloon. On Hong Kong Island it is Connaught Road, Des Voeux Road, Queen's Road and the roads between, with its concentration of shopping arcades, restaurants and offices. There are also plenty of shops in the malls and upper floors of the big complexes such as Prince's. Chinese goods are predominantly on sale in the streets leading up from Queen's Road Central, such as Wyndham Street, D'Aguilar Street and Wellington Street. In recent years the Causeway Bay district, between the Plaza, Excelsior and Lee Gardens Hotels, has developed into a good place to shop, particularly with its Japanese department stores, such as Daimaru, Mitsukoshi and Matsuzakaya, electronics shops and reasonably priced restaurants.
The main shopping in Kowloon is in the Tsimshatsui district and the harbor end of Nathan Road, where the streets running across it are lined with shops, restaurants and bars. Although there are also many more shops in the northern section of Nathan Road, in the more Chinese part of Kowloon, in Yaumati (west of Nathan Road and north of Jordan Road) and Mong Kok (both sides of Nathan Road and north of Waterloo Road) you may have difficulty in getting yourself understood. There are several hundred shops in the Ocean Terminal, selling all kinds of wares and it is worth looking at their displays. The Ocean Centre near by is also a big shopping center, leading over to Harbour City where there are yet more shops.
New on the Hong Kong shopping scene are the department stores on both sides of the harbor; these are operated by the People's Republic of China, and have goods ranging from household utensils to Chinese arts and crafts at fixed prices. The best known of these Chinese stores are Chinese Arts and Crafts (Wyndham Street, Central, Hong Kong and Salisbury Road, Kowloon), Yue Hwa (Kowloon) and Ching Kiu (Sai Yeung Choi Street, Mong Kok, Kowloon).
See Antiques, Department stores, Markets.

A selection of specialty shops:

Brassware

Ho Kwong Kee Metal Manufactory
Tung Nam Factory Building (1st floor)
A1–2, No. 40 Ma Tau Kok Road, Tokwawan, Kowloon

Hung Tai Brass Ware Factory
Wai Shun Industrial Building (8th floor)
5 Yuk Yat Street, Tokwawan, Kowloon

Cameras

Asia Photo Supply Ltd.
18 Carnarvon Road, Kowloon
5 Queen's Road Central, Hong Kong

	Broadway Photo Supply Ltd. 746 Nathan Road, Kowloon 3 Queen Victoria Street, Hong Kong
	Central Photo Supplies 314 Ocean Centre (3rd floor), Kowloon
	Kinefoto Ltd. Man Yee Building, Pottinger Street, Hong Kong
	Million Camera Co. Hyatt Regency Hotel, Kowloon
Carpets	*Tai Ping Carpet Factory Lot No. 1637, Ting Kok Road, Tai Po Market, New Territories (direction of Plover Cove Reservoir)
Carved ivory	*Kwong Fat Cheung Ivory and Mahjong Factory 27 Wellington Street, Hong Kong
	*Tack Cheung Ivory Factory 24 Wyndham Street, Hong Kong
	*Chams Ivory Factory Room 7, Haiphong Building (10th floor) Haiphong Road, Kowloon
Carved jade	Chu's Jade Factory 1A Kimberley New Street, Kowloon
Chinese lanterns	*Eastern Arts Plastic Co. Showroom: 20 Hennessy Road, Wanchai, Hong Kong Flat C, Tung Cheung Factory Building (8th floor) 653–659 King's Road, North Point, Hong Kong
Chinese paintings	*Harbour Village Star House (4th floor), Kowloon
	*Yee Tung Village Excelsior Shopping Arcade (2nd floor), Hong Kong
Electronics	Esquire Electronics Ltd. Ocean Centre, Kowloon Also cameras
	Excel Hi-Fi Co. 3 Pedder Street, Hong Kong
	The Camera and Hi-Fi People Ocean Terminal and Ocean Centre, Kowloon
	Tsang Fook Piano Co. Ocean Terminal, Kowloon
Jewelry	*Dennis Jewellery Manufacturers Kaiser Estate Building (4th floor), "H" 51 Man Yee Street, Hunghom, Kowloon
	*Tse Sui Luen Jewellery Co. Ltd. Head Office/Factory: Summit Building (ground floor) 30 Man Yue Street, Kowloon

Anju Jewellery Ltd.
Kaiser Estate Building, Block B2
41 Man Yue Street, Hunghom, Kowloon

Kay Tai Jewellery Co.
Furama Hotel, Hong Kong

Hongkong Artisans
Excelsior Hotel (1st floor), Hong Kong

Mahjong sets

William Ching Co.
60A Nathan Road, Kowloon

Painted china

Ah Chou Factory
10–18 Chun Pin Street (1st floor), Kwai Chung, New Territories

Tao Fung Shan, above Shatin (in the estate of the Tao Fung Shan Christian Institute)

Pearls

Pacific Pearls
926A Star House, Kowloon

Pewter

Ngan Hing Shum Co. Ltd.
Showroom:
112–116A Aplichau Gallery, Ocean Terminal, Kowloon
Factory:
Lot No. 3637, Shatin Lane, Ma Tau Wei Road, Kowloon

Porcelain and ceramics

Tung Fong (Porcelain & Ceramics) Ltd.
Flat B, 118 Kow Ming Street (4th floor), Kwun Tong, Kowloon

Sandalwood

Wing Lee Sandalwood Co.
409–411 Shanghai Street, Kowloon

Tailors and outfitters

A-MAN Hing Cheong (men's wear)
Mandarin Hotel, Hong Kong

Ascot Chang Co. Ltd. (men's shirts)
Peninsula Hotel, Kowloon

British Textile Co. (men and women)
Hilton Hotel, Hong Kong

Princeton (men and women)
201–210 Mary Building, 71–77 Peking Road, Kowloon

Shoong Salon de Mode (men and women)
25B Mody Road, Kowloon

Takley Custom Shirtmakers
Hilton Hotel, Hong Kong
Sheraton Hotel, Kowloon

Tak Tak Company (men and women)
Shop 38C, New World Centre, Kowloon
Regent Hotel, Kowloon

Zeepha Couture (women's wear)
12 Prince's Building, Hong Kong

Woodcarving and furniture

*Fortunate Arts and Furniture Ltd.
Showroom: 159 Tai Shan Gallery, Ocean Terminal, Kowloon
Factory: Golden Dragon Industrial Centre (24th floor), Block III, 172–180 Tai Lin Pai Road, Ha Kwai-Chung, New Territories

*Frank Yuen & Co. Ltd.
Showroom: 204 Ocean Terminal, Tsimshatsui, Kowloon
Factory: 60 Hung To Road (2nd floor), Kwun Tong, Kowloon

*J. L. George & Co. Ltd.
11 Kwai Tin Road (15th floor), Kwai Chung, New Territories

*Artistic Furniture Co.
Factory: Luen Ming Hing Factory Building
Flat B, 26 Mok Cheong Street, Tokwawan, Kowloon

Hai Feng Wood Arts Ltd.
Summit Building (4th floor)
Flat F, 30 Man Yue Street, Hunghom, Kowloon

Polly Handicrafts Company
Golden Dragon Industrial Centre (11th floor), Block 2, Flat L, 162–170 Tai Lin Pai Road, Ha Kwai Chang, New Territories

Macau

Macau's gold trade, which is subject to Government control, has quite a reputation, and each store displays the current price of gold. Prices for gold items are based on the day's gold price, plus workmanship and profit, so some bargaining is possible. Jewelry and precious metals should only be purchased from accredited members of the Macau Goldsmiths' Association, and Macau's Department of Tourism publishes a leaflet with addresses and general hints on shopping. See Information.
Macau's shops, which are open every day of the year except for a short break during or just after Chinese New Year, are mostly around the main street, Avenida Almeida Ribeiro, and goods tend often to be cheaper than in Hong Kong because of the lower overheads. There are antique shops in the city's backstreets, or around the Rua de Cinco de Outubro (see Antiques). They sell primarily Chinese and Colonial works of art. An extensive variety of contemporary Chinese arts and crafts can also be obtained. Many shops in Macau sell men's and women's sports and casual clothes at bargain prices, particularly around the Rua Palha and at the stalls at the S. Domingos Market and along Cinco de Outubro.

Sightseeing tours

Coach tours

Most hotels have a desk which can give information about sightseeing tours by coach and can take reservations. Several such tours are run daily by various travel agencies, including general sightseeing tours, special interest tours and "Hong Kong by night" tours. A meal is usually included in the price.

Hong Kong Tourist Association

The Hong Kong Tourist Association issues an orange folder listing the tours on offer.
Information about tours can be obtained from the Association's branches at the Airport, the Star Ferry Concourse in Kowloon, the Government Publications Centre in the General Post

Office Building, the Connaught Centre (35th floor) and the World Trade Centre (see Information). Telephone information service: dial 3–671111.

Sightseeing by car

One very comfortable and convenient way of sightseeing is to hire a car, with driver. This costs more, but has the advantage that the tour can be tailor-made to your own personal requirements. Information about chauffeur-driven car hire can be obtained from hotels or the Hong Kong Tourist Association.
See Boat travel.

Hong Kong

There are a great many tour operators in Hong Kong offering a very varied program of sightseeing tours. Anyone wanting a preliminary tour to get to know Hong Kong Island would do well to take one of the tours lasting three to four hours and including Victoria Peak and Aberdeen Harbour. There are also half-day tours through the New Territories, with a trip to the Chinese border, as well as various trips around the harbor.
See Travel agencies.
The China Tour Centre runs trips into the People's Republic of China (614 New World Centre; offices in the Imperial, Regal Meridien and Harbour View Hotels).
Gray Line Tours of Hong Kong, 501 Cheong Hing Building, 72 Nathan Road, Kowloon, tel. 3–687111, organizes tours both within Hong Kong and to Macau and the People's Republic of China. Various kinds of ferries run from Hong Kong's Macau Terminal to Macau in the west (see Ferries).

Helicopter flights

Heliservices provide flights out over the harbor, the islands and the New Territories to the Chinese frontier for up to 4 persons, 5–45 minutes, in a Bell 206B Jetranger. Information and reservations through the Hong Kong Tourist Association (see Information).

Macau

Many tour operators provide sightseeing in both Macau and Hong Kong. Tour operators include:
Able, tel. 89798
Asia, tel. 96287 (Hong Kong 3–693847)
China Travel Service, tel. 88922 – specialists in day-tours to China
Estoril, tel. 573614 (Hong Kong 5–443879)
Hi No De Caravela, tel. 77272
H. Nolasco, tel. 76463
International, tel. 86522 (Hong Kong 5–443879) – specialists in 1–5 day excursions to China
Lotus, tel. 81765
Macau, tel. 85555 (Hong Kong 3–661158)
Macau Zhuhai, tel. 76586
MBC Tours, tel. 76422
Sintra, tel. 86394 (Hong Kong 5–237141/2)
South China, tel. 87211
S.D.T.M., tel. 75164 (Hong Kong 5–437297)
T.K.W., tel. 76200
Wing On, tel. 77701
See Travel agencies.
For reservations made in Hong Kong the firm in question will also take care of the visa, ferry tickets and trip from the harbor to the hotel.

People's Republic of China

The International Tourism Agency based in Hong Kong (tel. Macau 86522, Hong Kong 5–412011) organizes excursions into China, including Canton. The program includes visits to a school or commune, a market city, the birthplace of Sun Yat-sen and several museums.

Sport

Hong Kong
Various Hong Kong sports clubs offer visitors temporary membership so that they can use their facilities for a fee.

Basketball

This is a very popular sport in Hong Kong and played in many places.

Cricket

During the cooler season there are weekend matches at the Hong Kong Cricket Club, Gap Road, Wongneichong.

Football

Football is also very popular, with frequent friendly matches between the various clubs.

Golf

The Royal Hong Kong Golf Club in Fanling, New Territories, has three 18-hole golf courses. Visitors may normally only play Monday to Friday. Information can be obtained from the Club Secretary, tel. 5–233233. There is also a 9-hole course at Deep Water Bay.

Horse-racing

The horse-racing season runs from September to May. The Royal Hong Kong Jockey Club operates two racetracks – Happy Valley (see Hong Kong A to Z) and, the newer of the two, Sha Tin. Meetings are normally on Saturday evenings and Wednesday afternoons. Racegoers should get there in good time for the start. Access to the members' stands is through the Off-Course Betting Centre. Guests should bring their passports if they want a visitor's ticket.

Rugby

The very good rugby team plays its matches in the winter (September–May) on Wednesday evenings and Saturday afternoons.

Skating

There are skating rinks in the Lai Chi Kok Amusement Park and in Hong Kong Island's City Plaza.

Squash and tennis

There are tennis and squash courts at most of the big hotels, as well as in Victoria Park, Hong Kong Island, and Tsai Park, Kowloon.

Swimming

The Crown Colony has 38 public bathing beaches which tend to get very crowded at the weekend.
See Bathing beaches and Swimming-pools.

Walking

There are a great many walks and paths outside the built-up areas. For the adventurous there is the 60 miles or so of the Mac Lehose Trail through the particularly lovely landscapes of the New Territories, taking in parts of eight country parks and divided up into ten sections. Bus stops at regular intervals make it easier to chose which stretches you want to walk, making it possible to cover a considerable distance in daily stages.

Sports Tours

The Hong Kong Tourist Association now also offers a Sports and Recreation Tour where you can be collected from your hotel, have lunch at the sports club and be returned to your hotel. Sports equipment can be hired at the clubs.

Information on mountaineering, sailing, water-skiing, scuba-diving, horseback riding, tennis, squash, etc. can be obtained from the Hong Kong Tourist Association.

Sports grounds and stadia

Hong Kong Government Stadium
Soo Kun Poo, Causeway Bay, Hong Kong

Hong Kong Football Club Grounds
Sports Road, Happy Valley, Hong Kong

Mong Kok Stadium
Flower Market Road, Mong Kok, Kowloon

South China Athletic Grounds
Caroline Hill, Causeway Bay, Hong Kong

Queen Elizabeth Stadium
Morrison Hill, Happy Valley, Hong Kong

Hong Kong Coliseum (previously Hung Hom Stadium)
Hung Hom, Kowloon

Jubilee Sports Centre
Sha Tin, New Territories

See Fitness centres.

Macau

Canidrome

Greyhound-racing takes place at 8 p.m. at the Canidrome on weekends and public holidays (see Macau A to Z).

Horse-racing

Trotting races at the Taipa track are a popular local sport, using primarily Australian horses and trainers. The Sunday races start at 1.30 p.m.

Jai-Alai

Jai-Alai, supposedly the fastest ball-game in the world, is a great attraction for tourists. The stadium is near the hovercraft terminal. The games at weekends take place from 2 p.m.; otherwise they start at 7.30 p.m. (see Macau A to Z).

Marathons

Macau has several marathons.

Motor-racing

The Macau Grand Prix is the highpoint of the sporting calendar. It forms part of the Formula III World Championship and takes place in mid-November. There is also motorcycle and saloon car racing.

Swimming-pools

Swimming is the most popular sport in Hong Kong, in summer. Hong Kong has ten public swimming-pools run by the municipal authorities, two of which (at Aberdeen and Tai Wan Shan) are 50 meters long. In addition, there are, at present,

three more swimming-pools in the New Territories, managed by the New Territories Services Department. Twenty-three new swimming-pool complexes are planned, and at least one is already under construction at Lai Chi Kok. There is one heated indoor pool at Morrison Hill. There are also other swimming-pools at Victoria Bay and Kowloon Tsai. Information: tel. 5–95590.
See Bathing beaches.

Telegrams and telephone services

Telegrams
Telegrams and telexes can be handed in at the Cable and Wireless offices listed below, and hotels will also arrange to send them for you, but will charge a fee for doing so.

Telephone services

Local calls

Local calls are free, though there are a few coin-operated telephones in public buildings and hotel lobbies which require payment to be made even for a local call. Any such calls made from a hotel room are not charged on the bill. If you have occasion to telephone when in Hong Kong, do as the locals do: pick up a telephone, without asking permission, in any restaurant, shop or office you are in. Most establishments have instruments for the use of the public.

Overseas calls

International calls can only be made through hotel switchboards (for which a service charge is usually made), Hermes House (24-hour service, tel. 3–7220097), Sutherland House (24-hour service, tel. 5–237439), Lee Gardens (tel. 5–770577), or the Cable and Wireless Company's offices, with payment in advance. For local information dial 108. A 3-minute call to Europe costs about HK$55/150 patacas.

International codes

Hong Kong 852 followed by area code for
Hong Kong Island 5
Kowloon 3
Lantau 5
New Territories 0
followed by customer's number

Macau 853 followed by customer's number

Cable and Wireless offices:

New Mercury House, Gloucester Road, Hong Kong
tel. 5–283111
Open 8 a.m.–midnight

Mercury House
Connaught Road (near Furama Hotel), Hong Kong
tel. 5–237435
Open 24 hours a day

Ocean Terminal, Kowloon
tel. 3–664063
Open 7.30 a.m.–midnight

Kai Tak Airport, Kowloon
tel. 3-8297914
Open Mon.–Sat. 8.30 a.m.–10 p.m., Sun. noon–7 p.m.

Television

See Radio and television.

Ticket agencies

City Hall

Tickets for events in City Hall can be obtained from the City Hall box office in Edinburgh Place (tel. 5-229928 and 5-229511).

Hong Kong Arts Centre

For tickets for events in the Hong Kong Arts Centre (tel. 5-280626) apply to:

Hong Kong Arts Centre Box Office
2 Harbour Road, Wanchai, Hong Kong

South China Morning Post Family Bookshop
Canton House, 54 Queen's Road Central, Hong Kong

Shop 313
Ocean Centre (3rd floor), Kowloon

Other events

Tickets for other events are usually obtainable from:

Tom Lee Piano Company
6 Cameron Road, Kowloon, tel. 3-661704
60 Des Voeux Road Central, Hong Kong, tel. 5-230934

Time

Hong Kong and Macau both observe Hong Kong Standard Time which is constant all year round, and is 8 hours ahead of Greenwich Mean Time and 13 hours ahead of US Eastern Standard Time.

Tipping

Hotels and restaurants

Most hotels and restaurants add a service charge of 10 per cent to the bill. It is usual, however, to add another 5–10 per cent when paying the bill in a restaurant, and to give something to room staff and the porter when leaving a hotel.

Hairdressers, taxi-drivers, etc.

In the case of other services (hairdressers, taxi-drivers, etc.) a tip of 5–10 per cent is expected.

Porters

Porters carrying luggage at airports and hotels should be given HK$1 per piece.

Toilets

Public toilets fall short of European and North American standards and should be avoided. The cleanest toilets are to be found in hotels; those in department stores are also usually acceptable.

Travel agencies

Hong Kong

American Express International Inc.
37 Queen's Road Central, Hong Kong, tel. 5–210211

Eupo Air Travel Service (HK) Ltd.
Room 1905, Wing On Centre
Connaught Road Central, Hong Kong, tel. 5–434171

Firebird Travel Services Ltd.
Room 1235, Star House, Kowloon, tel. 3–699633

Jardines Airways Division
Alexandra House (30th floor), Hong Kong, tel. 5–228011

Pegasus Travel (HK) Ltd.
Fu House, Ice House Street, Hong Kong, tel. 5–265677

Sunbird Travel Centre Ltd.
5 Middle Road, Kowloon, tel. 3–681847

Swire Travel
Swire House (2nd floor)
9 Connaught Road Central, Hong Kong, tel. 5–256081

Thomas Cook Overseas Ltd.
Gammon House (9th floor), Central, Hong Kong
tel. 5–235151

Westminster Travel Ltd.
1129 Star House, Kowloon, tel. 3–695051

Macau

Able
"C" (ground floor)
5–9 Travessa do Pe. Narciso, Ed. Hoi Kwong, tel. 89798

Asia
23A–B Rua da Praia Grande, tel. 82687

China Travel Service
63–63A Rua da Praia Grande, tel. 573770, 88812, 88922

Estoril
Hotel Lisboa (ground floor), tel. 573614

International
9B Travessa do Pe. Narciso (ground floor)
tel. 86522, 87884, 86567

Hi-No-De Caravela Lda.
Hotel Matsuya, Estrada de S. Francisco, tel. 77272

Lotus
Edifício Fong Meng (ground floor), Rua de S. Lourenço
tel. 81765

Macau
9 Ave. da Amizade, tel. 85555

Macau Zhuhai
16–22 Rua Dr. Pedro José Lobo, tel. 75460

*H. Nolasco & Cia. Lda.
20 Ave. Almeida Ribeiro, tel. 76463, 76472, 573738

South China
Apartment B (1st floor), 15A–B Ave. Dr. Rodrigo Rodrigues
tel. 87211, 87219

S.T.D.M.
Hotel Sintra, Room 207, tel. 85878

T.K.W.
Apartment 408 (4th floor), 27–31 Rua Formosa, tel. 76200

Travel documents

Passport

All visitors to Hong Kong must have a valid passport, with at least six months to go before expiry.
Under a law introduced in November 1980 to control illegal immigration it is obligatory to carry an identity document at all times. Visitors may, therefore, be asked at any time to produce their passport to a police officer. Failure to do so is an offence which may attract heavy penalties (maximum fine HK$1000, with the possibility of a prison sentence for repeated offences).

Visa

No visa is required by United Kingdom nationals for a stay of up to 6 months, other Commonwealth citizens for up to 3 months or United States citizens for up to one month.
All visitors arriving by air must have tickets for their return or onward flight. Young visitors in particular may be asked to produce evidence that they have sufficient means for their stay in the colony.

Residence permit

If you intend to stay in Hong Kong for any considerable time you should apply in advance to the immigration authorities for a residence permit.

Immigration Department, International Building (14th and 15th floors), Des Voeux Road Central, Hong Kong, tel. 5-456065.

Inoculations

No inoculations are required for entry to Hong Kong except for persons who have been in a smallpox or cholera infected area within the previous 14 days. Such persons must have a valid international vaccination certificate. As the regulations in force can be changed at short notice it is advisable to check with the official tourist organization (see Information) or your travel agent immediately before departure. The immigration authorities in Macau work on the assumption that all health certificates that may be required have already been examined on arrival in Hong Kong.

Representation of Hong Kong in other countries

Hong Kong is represented abroad by British embassies, consulates and (in Commonwealth countries) High Commissions, from which information about entry regulations can be obtained.

Weather forecasts

The English-language radio stations give weather forecasts every hour (Commercial Radio every half-hour), and on the television services there is a weather forecast after every news bulletin. Forecasts are also published in the newspapers.
During the typhoon season (June–September) there are frequent announcements, when a typhoon warning is in force, on the weather situation, the state of traffic and any holdups due to flooding or landslides.
On average, about 30 cyclones a year arise in the sea areas near Hong Kong. Of these, about 15 reach typhoon intensity. Few threaten Hong Kong itself and when that happens various routine precautions are taken to minimize the damage and danger to the public.

Weights and measures

Hong Kong has recently gone metric, somethig that Macau as a Portuguese-governed territory has always been, but British and some traditional Chinese weights and measures are still also in general use.

Length and area

1 inch=2·54 cm
1 foot=0·305 m
1 acre=0·405 hectares
1 mile=1·609 km
1 square mile=2·59 km^2
1 cubic foot=0·028 m^3

Weight

1 pound=453 g
1 ounce=28·35 g
1 pound=16 ounces

Capacity

1 gallon=4·54 litres
1 quart=1·135 litres
1 pint=0·5675 litre
1 gallon=4 quarts
1 quart=2 pints

Chinese weights and measures

With the exception of the tael (1 tael (or "leung")=38 g approx.) and the catty (1 catty (or "kan")=0·6 kg approx.), the old Chinese weights and measures are now rare, though the "chek" or Chinese foot (=0·37 m) is still used by some Chinese.

Weights

The smallest unit of weight is the fun.
10 funs=1 chin
10 chins=1 tael or leung ($1\frac{1}{3}$ oz)
16 taels=1 catty or gun ($1\frac{1}{3}$ lb)
100 catties=1 dam or picul (133 lb)

Measures of length

The tsün (1·312 inches) is the Chinese inch.
The chek (1·0936 feet) is the Chinese foot.
The lay (0·3107 mile) is the Chinese mile.

When to go to Hong Kong

See Facts and Figures, Climate.

Youth hostels

Hong Kong

Reservations can be made through the head office of the Hong Kong Youth Hostels Association, Room 1408, Block "A", Watson's Estate, North Point, Hong Kong, tel. 5–706222/3. This office can also give information about closing times. Most hostels are closed between 10 a.m. and 4 p.m., with lights out at 11 p.m.
Visitors can do their own cooking free of charge since meals are seldom available. There is no age limit; bedding can be obtained on request.

Bradbury Hall
Bradbury Hall, Chek Keng, Sai Kung Peninsula, New Territories; 100 b., tel. 3–282458

Cambrai Lodge
Nim Wan, Lau Fau Shan, New Territories; 28 b.
Open only at weekends and during vacations.

Ma Wui Hall
Top of Mount Davis, Hong Kong Island; 112 b., tel. 5–8175715

Mong Tun Wan
Mong Tun Wan YH, Lantau Island; 88 b., tel. 5–9841389

Ngong Ping
Lantau Islands; 48 b., tel. 5–9857610

Pak Sha-O
Pak Sha-O, Jones Cove, Sai Kung Peninsula; 116 b., tel. 3–282327
This hostel has facilities for wheelchair-users.

Sze Lok Yuen
Tai Mo Shan, Tsuen Wan, New Territories; 80 b., tel. 0–988188

Wayfoong Hall
Plover Cove, Ting Kok Road, Tai Po, New Territories; 110 b., tel. 0–6568323

Macau

On Cheoc Van Beach, Coloane Island.

Useful Telephone Numbers

Emergencies	
– Fire, police, medical emergency	999
– Hospital treatment (outpatient)	5–746211
– Breakdown service at night (HKAA)	5–737474
– Police visitor's hotline	5–277177
Information	
– Tourist offices:	
China Travel Service	5–259121
Hong Kong Tourist Information Service	3–7225555
Macau Tourist Information Bureau	3–677747
Watertours of Hong Kong Ltd. (boat trips)	5–254808
– Events:	
City Hall	5–229928
Hong Kong Arts Centre	5–271122
British Council	5–756501
Hong Kong Automobile Association (HKAA)	5–737474
Airlines	
– British Airways	5–775023
– British Caledonian	5–212353
– Cathay Pacific	5–252202, 3–662407
– Pan American	5–231111, 3–687171
Ferries	
– Far East Hydrofoil Company (to Macau)	5–457021
– Hong Kong and Yaumati Ferry (Hong Kong and islands)	5–423081
– Hong Kong Macau Hydrofoil Co. Ltd.	5–2118302
– Sealink Ferries Ltd.	5–423081
– Hong Kong Hi-Speed Ferries Ltd.	5–8152299
Diplomatic missions	
– United Kingdom	5–230176
– Canada	5–282222
– Australia	5–227171
– New Zealand	5–255044
– United States	5–239011
Lost property	
– Police	5–284284
– Public transport:	
China Motor Bus Co.	5–616171
Hong Kong Tramways	5–764321
Kowloon Motor Bus Co.	12–296161
Kowloon–Canton Railway	3–646321
Mass Transit Railways	3–7585111
Peak Tramway	5–220922
Telephone	
– Dialling codes within Hong Kong:	
Hong Kong Island to Kowloon	3
Hong Kong Island to New Territories	10
Kowloon to Hong Kong Island	5
Kowloon to New Territories	10
New Territories to Hong Kong Island	5
New Territories to Kowloon	3
– International dialling codes	100, 101

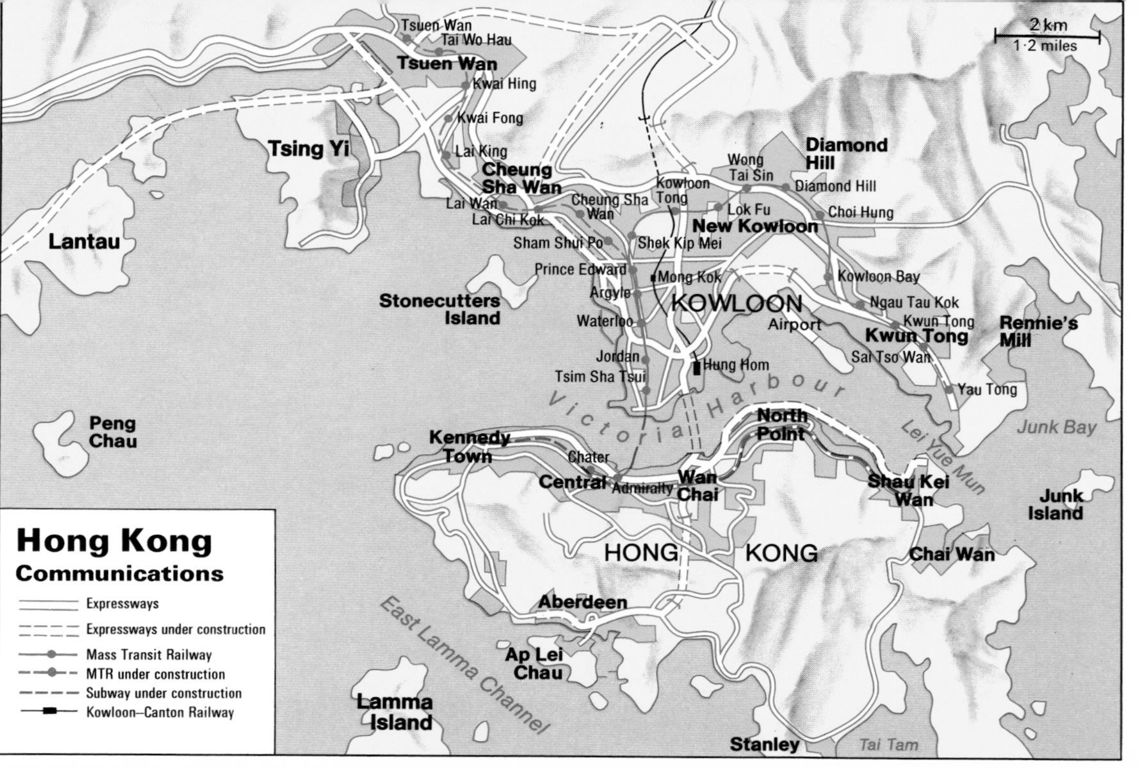

Hong Kong
Communications
Expressways
Expressways under construction
Mass Transit Railway
MTR under construction
Subway under construction
Kowloon–Canton Railway
2 km
1·2 miles
Tsuen Wan
Tai Wo Hau
Tsuen Wan
Kwai Hing
Kwai Fong
Lai King
Tsing Yi
Cheung Sha Wan
Lai Wan
Lai Chi Kok
Cheung Sha Wan
Sham Shui Po
Lantau
Wong Tai Sin
Diamond Hill
Diamond Hill
Kowloon Tong
Lok Fu
Choi Hung
New Kowloon
Shek Kip Mei
Prince Edward
Mong Kok
Kowloon Bay
Argyle
KOWLOON
Ngau Tau Kok
Stonecutters Island
Waterloo
Airport
Kwun Tong
Kwun Tong
Rennie's Mill
Sai Tso Wan
Jordan
Hung Hom
Tsim Sha Tsui
Yau Tong
Victoria Harbour
North Point
Junk Bay
Lei Yue Mun
Peng Chau
Kennedy Town
Chater
Central
Admiralty
Wan Chai
Shau Kei Wan
Junk Island
HONG KONG
Chai Wan
Aberdeen
East Lamma Channel
Ap Lei Chau
Lamma Island
Stanley
Tai Tam

Notes

Notes

Notes

A series of city guides filled with colour photographs and detailed maps and floor plans from one of the oldest names in travel publishing:

Please send me the books checked below:

- ☐ **Amsterdam** $10.95
  0-13-057969-6
- ☐ **Athens** $10.95
  0-13-057977-7
- ☐ **Bangkok** $10.95
  0-13-057985-8
- ☐ **Berlin** $10.95
  0-13-367996-9
- ☐ **Brussels** $10.95
  0-13-368788-0
- ☐ **Copenhagen** $10.95
  0-13-057993-9
- ☐ **Florence** $10.95
  0-13-369505-0
- ☐ **Frankfurt** $10.95
  0-13-369570-0
- ☐ **Hamburg** $10.95
  0-13-369687-1
- ☐ **Hong Kong** $10.95
  0-13-058009-0
- ☐ **Jerusalem** $10.95
  0-13-058017-1
- ☐ **London** $10.95
  0-13-058025-2
- ☐ **Madrid** $10.95
  0-13-058033-3
- ☐ **Moscow** $10.95
  0-13-058041-4
- ☐ **Munich** $10.95
  0-13-370370-3
- ☐ **New York** $10.95
  0-13-058058-9
- ☐ **Paris** $10.95
  0-13-058066-X
- ☐ **Rome** $10.95
  0-13-058074-0
- ☐ **San Francisco** $10.95
  0-13-058082-1
- ☐ **Singapore** $10.95
  0-13-058090-2
- ☐ **Tokyo** $10.95
  0-13-058108-9
- ☐ **Venice** $10.95
  0-13-058116-X
- ☐ **Vienna** $10.95
  0-13-371303-2

PRENTICE HALL PRESS

Order Department—Travel Books

200 Old Tappan Road

Old Tappan, New Jersey 07675

In U.S. include $1 postage and handling for 1st book, 25¢ each additional book. Outside U.S. $2 and 50¢ respectively.

Enclosed is my check or money order for $__________

NAME__________

ADDRESS__________

CITY__________ STATE______ ZIP______